KB270639

처음 시작하는 한국어 기초문법
Survival Korean Basic Grammar Skills

지은이 Stephen Revere
펴낸이 **안용백**
펴낸곳 (주)넥서스

초판 1쇄 발행 2007년 4월 5일
초판 5쇄 발행 2014년 8월 20일

2판 1쇄 인쇄 2015년 8월 10일
2판 1쇄 발행 2015년 8월 25일

출판신고 1992년 4월 3일 제311-2002-2호
121-840 서울시 마포구 양화로 8길 24
Tel (02)330-5500 Fax (02)330-5555

ISBN 979-11-5752-347-4 18740

www.nexusbook.com

Stephen Revere · 진제희

넥서스

Preface

When I set out to write the original *Survival Korean*, I learned a difficult lesson – writing a book, especially a language book, takes about 10 times more work than you think it will. At the time I thought, "Write the dialogs and explain them. How hard can that be?" I laugh at my naiveté now. Making the dialogs natural, but including all the grammar and vocabulary that you want to teach; avoiding including things you haven't explained yet; recycling things you have already explained; organizing, editing, etc. – it was a massive project. But I was incredibly lucky. As a proofreader I was able to get Jae-hee Jin, my graduate school 선배 (senior). Despite receiving a pittance for all her diligent work, she was absolutely meticulous in making sure that everything was perfect. She had a great hand in making the original Survival Korean a success. That's why I knew she had to be coauthor on my next book – proper compensation for working on the first book as well as knowing that she would make a great contribution to the new book.

I'm the first Westerner to graduate with a degree in Teaching Korean as a Foreign Language, but Jae-hee is the first person to graduate with a degree in Teaching Korean as a Foreign Language, along with two classmates. She started the degree when Yonsei University started the program for the first time in 1997. She is also the first **person** from our program to go on to get a PhD and go back to become a professor teaching in the program where we were both formerly students. I was born in the year of the pig, and in Korea they say that pigs have a lot of 인복 – 'people luck.' It's certainly true in my case.

Stephen Revere

The last year spent preparing this book has been an extremely rewarding experience. In that time I have been able to learn more about the perspective that foreign students bring to Korean language learning. Having taught Korean to foreign learners for over 10 years, I thought I knew pretty well how foreign students viewed the language. Working with Stephen, however, has helped me gain a more thorough experience and even greater understanding of the perspective of foreign students of Korean.

The reason that both the original Survival Korean and the Survival Korean: Basic Grammar Skills provide the learner with an insightful and interesting learning opportunity is that they are both written from the perspective of a foreigner who has learned Korean as well as a person who has received a Master's Degree in Teaching Korean and personally taught Korean to students from various countries and backgrounds. This grammar book in particular displays differences in perspective and teaching methodology that make it completely different from other Korean books previously written.

In the end, this book helps give the Korean learner a sense of comfort as well as build interest in the language. Students will find that they are able to finally solve the many aspects of Korean that may have perplexed them in the past.

I developed a great friendship with Stephen as his graduate school colleague in Teaching Korean as a Second Language. Now, I would like to sincerely thank him for the opportunity he has gladly offered me to be his co-author as well.

Jae-hee Jin

Now that we've got the mutual admiration society meeting out of the way, Jae-hee and I would like to thank Nexus Publishing for caring so much about Korean education. Specifically we want to thank So-yeon Seo for her hard work on this book. She had many late evenings at the office working on this book and that work is very much appreciated. We would also like to thank our professors at Yonsei, especially Ha-soo Kim, Bong-ja Baek, and Seung-hae Kang. They were teaching students of Korean before it was popular. The truly practical education that they gave us made this book what it is. We will be forever grateful for their tutelage.

Stephen Revere and Jae-hee Jin

How to Use This Book

Survival Korean **Basic Grammar Skills** is designed to expose you to a single grammar form to such a large extent that it becomes a habit. While the first *Survival Korean* book was intended to naturally expose you to the most frequent and useful Korean expressions in context, we wrote **Basic Grammar Skills** to drive home the basic usage of each expression - which can often be surprisingly diverse. While the focus of the original book was receptive skills, the focus of this book is production; we want to make sure that you understand the usage and can use the given expressions.

There is not necessarily a specific order in which you should do this book. For the most part the book doesn't get more difficult as it goes along - it is the same level of vocabulary and grammar usage from beginning to end. And we didn't want difficult vocabulary to get in the way of understanding the grammar. That is why there is an **Essential Vocabulary** list at the very beginning of this book. These are the most common and necessary words in the Korean language, and we avoided using any words in the grammar descriptions that are not on the list. If you know all of the words on that short list, then you will be able to do this entire book without vocabulary words getting in the way.

Each chapter starts out with a visualization of the specific vocabulary in the format that it is used. If the grammar point is attached to nouns then you will see it attached to an N. If there has to be a space then you will see a space in the middle. Then there is a very basic explanation of the conjugation or the usage of the grammar point. That is followed up by a plain-English explanation of the grammar and a few basic examples with pictures and translation.

The second section is **Extension**. It is filled with numerous examples of the different ways each specific grammar point can be used. They are not translated for you, but instead you are given a sentence to help you figure out the meaning of the sentence on your own if you don't know all the vocabulary in the sentence already. It may be a response to the sentence, or a naturally following next sentence, etc. In this way you can translate the sentences yourself first and then check the answers at the back to make sure your translation was right.

Then comes the **Skills Building**. This section starts out with a listening exercise to practice your receptive skills first. Then it's your turn. Diverse practice exercises are given to make sure that you can produce the grammar yourself. By the time you have completed each chapter, you will have seen or produced copious examples for each grammar point.

As you can see, this is a beginner's book designed to take you to the next level. You may have seen this stuff before or you may not have, but if you complete this book you'll be able to use every expression given. It's designed to make sure that by the time you're done, you'll be a beginner no more. This way you can survive - and even thrive - in Korea.

A few things you should know before you get started. A 받침 is a final consonant to a syllable, and if you're not sure what it is you may want to pick up the original *Survival Korean* for a more detailed explanation. Also you will see letters substituted for words quite often. 'N' stands for noun, 'V' stands for verb, 'A' stands for adjective, 'P' stands for person and 'Pl' is for place.

Contents

Essential Vocabulary

Personal Information 개인 정보

이름 name	나이 age
살 years old	주소 address
남자 boy, man	여자 girl, woman
생일 birthday	

Transportation 교통

지하철 subway, metro	자동차, 차 automobile, car
자전거 bicycle	오토바이 motorcycle
비행기 airplane	기차 train
KTX 'Korean Train Express'	

Furniture 가구

침대 bed	책상 desk
의자 chair	

Clothing and Accessories 옷과 액세서리

바지 pants(반바지 shorts)	치마 skirt
신발 shoes	운동화 exercise shoes
구두 dress shoes	모자 hat
안경 glasses	시계 watch
넥타이 a necktie	가방 bag
지갑 wallet	장갑 gloves

Body 몸

얼굴 face	눈 eye(s)
입 mouth	코 nose
팔 arm(s)	다리 leg(s)
머리 head/hair	손 hand(s)

Places and Stores 장소와 가게

공항 airport	우체국 post office
바닷가 beach	방 room
병원 hospital	은행 bank
서점 bookstore	편의점 convenience store

술집 bar
슈퍼(마켓) supermarket
시장 open market
식당 restaurant
지하철역 metro station
집 house

커피숍 coffee shop
극장, 영화관 theater
백화점 department store
회사 company, office
기차역 train station
화장실 bathroom

School 학교

학생 student
유치원 kindergarten
중학교 middle school
대학교 university
수업 class
방학 school vacation

선생님 teacher
초등학교 primary school
고등학교 high school
도서관 library
숙제 homework
입학 entrance into a school

Meals 식사

아침 breakfast (morning)
저녁 dinner (evening)

점심 lunch

Drinks 음료

홍차 black tea (lit. red tea)
인삼차 ginseng tea
맥주 beer
소주 soju (Korean spirit)
콜라 coke

녹차 green tea
우유 milk
술 alcohol
사이다 lemon soda

Fruits, Vegetables and Grains 과일, 채소와 곡식

밥 rice
딸기 strawberries
당근 carrot
상추 lettuce
고추 red pepper

사과 apple
수박 water melon
양파 onion
마늘 garlic

Meat 고기

소 cow
닭 chicken

돼지 pig
고기 meat

소고기 beef
닭고기 chicken
생선 fish (for eating)

돼지고기 pork
물고기 fish (in a pond)
생선회 raw fish

Korean Foods 한국 음식

불고기 marinated beef
김치 kimchi
삼계탕 ginseng chicken soup

갈비 marinated ribs
된장찌개 fermented bean-paste stew
닭갈비 stir-fried chicken and vegetables

비빔밥 various vegetables mixed with rice and Korean red pepper paste

Ingredients 재료

계란 egg
설탕 sugar
후추 pepper

빵 bread
소금 salt
고추장 red pepper paste

Things to Read 읽을 것

책 book
잡지 magazine

신문 newspaper
편지 letter

Colors 색깔

하얀색 white
빨간색 red
녹색 green

검은색 black
파란색 blue
노란색 yellow

Entertainment 엔터테인먼트

영화 movie
음악 music
노래 a song

공연 performance
춤 dance

Machines 기계

전화 telephone
컴퓨터 computer

휴대전화 mobile phone

Jobs 직업

간호사 nurse
회사원 business person
택시기사 taxi driver

의사 doctor
교수 professor

Family 가족

할머니 grandmother	할아버지 grandfather
어머니, 엄마 mother, mom	아버지, 아빠 father, dad
부모(님) parents	동생 younger sibling
언니, 누나 older sister	오빠, 형 older brother
남편 husband	아내, 부인 wife
딸 daughter	아들 son
아이 kid	

Languages and Countries 언어와 나라

한국 Korea	한국말, 한국어 Korean language
일본 Japan	일본말, 일본어 Japanese langauge
중국 China	중국말, 중국어 Chinese language
독일 Germany	독일말, 독일어 German language
영국 England	영어 English
미국 America	

Activities 활동 (all of these activities are made into verbs by adding 하다)

운동 exercise	일 work
공부 study	수영 swimming
등산 hiking	축구 soccer
야구 baseball	요리 cooking

Weather and Seasons 날씨와 계절

비 rain	눈 snow
바람 wind	봄 spring
여름 summer	가을 fall
겨울 winter	

Time 시간

시간 hour	분 minutes
일 day	주 week (주말 weekend)
월 month	년 year
월요일 Monday	화요일 Tuesday
수요일 Wednesday	목요일 Thursday
금요일 Friday	토요일 Saturday
일요일 Sunday	요즘 these days

어제 yesterday   오늘 today
내일 tomorrow   이번 this time
지난 last   다음 next
아침 morning   밤 night
오전 morning, a.m.   오후 afternoon, p.m.
매(일, 주, 월, 년) every(day, week, month, year)

Basic Adverbs 부사

열심히 hard, diligently   푹 completely (used only with rest or sleep)
잘 well   빨리 quick(ly)
보통 usually   많이 a lot
같이 together   혼자 alone
처음 for the first time   지금 now
자주 often   가끔 sometimes
더 more   제일 the most
아직 not yet   늦게 about
다시 again   잠깐(만) for a moment
이따가 a little later   금방 soon

Emphasis 강조

아주 very   정말 really
너무 too   좀, 조금 a little bit, please

Postpositions of Location 장소 부사

앞에 in front of   뒤에 behind
위에 over, above   밑에, 아래에 below, under
안에 inside   밖에 outside
옆에 next to   사이에 between
오른쪽에 on the right   왼쪽에 on the left
근처에 nearby, in the neighborhood

Misc. Stuff 기타 것

가격 price   그렇지만 but
그리고 and   그런데 however, by the way
감기 a cold   국 broth
돈 money   대통령 president
곳 place   미팅 blind date

문제 problem
구경 seeing, sightseeing
나무 tree
단어 word
물 water
시내 downtown
약 medicine
월급 salary
인기 popularity
거짓말 a lie
창문 window
표 ticket(s)
사람 person
손님 customer
선배 senior, older friend

동네 the neighborhood
열쇠 key(s)
수저 spoon and chopsticks
선물 present
연필 pencil
인기 popularity
아줌마 married woman
생각 idea, thought
질문 question
친구 friend
꽃 flower
외국인, 외국사람 foreigner
휴가 vacation
후배 junior, younger friend

Basic Verbs 기본 동사

가다 to go
보다 to watch
타다 to ride
나가다 to go out
자다 to sleep
닫다 to close
찾다 to look for, find
먹다 to eat
주다 to give
보내다 to send
읽다 to read
늦다 to be late
믿다 to believe
가르치다 to teach
다니다 to attend
하다 to do
말하다 to talk
연락하다 to contact
일하다 to work
도착하다 to arrive

오다 to come
끝나다 to end, finish
만나다 to meet
나오다 to come out
사다 to buy
받다 to receive
맞다 to fit
웃다 to laugh, smile
배우다 to learn
싸우다 to fight
잊다 to forget
웃기다 to be funny
마시다 to drink
기다리다 to wait
쉬다 to rest
걱정하다 to worry
운전하다 to drive
시작하다 to begin, start
여행하다 to travel
출발하다 to depart

예매하다 to purchase in advance
주문하다 to make an order
좋아하다 to like
주차하다 to park (a car)
청소하다 to clean
샤워하다 to take a show
물어보다 to ask

이야기하다 to talk
회의하다 to have a meeting
싫어하다 to hate
준비하다 to prepare
쇼핑하다 to shop
도와주다 to help

To wear, put on 입다, 쓰다

입다 to wear, put on (clothes)
신다 to wear, put on (footwear)
차다 to wear, put on (watch)

쓰다 to wear, put on (hat, glasses)
하다 to wear, put on (jewelry)

Noun-Verb pairs

노래를 부르다, 하다 to sing a song
담배를 피우다 to smoke a cigarette
시계를 차다 to wear a watch
춤을 추다 to dance (a dance)
테니스를 치다 to play tennis

마음에 들다 to like
사진을 찍다 to take a picture
시간이 걸리다 to take time
친구를 사귀다 to make a friend
화가 나다 to get angry

Basic Adjectives 기본 형용사

같다 to be same
많다 to be a lot
싸다 to be cheap
맑다 to be clear
적다 to be few, small in amount
흐리다 to be cloudy
따뜻하다 to do
피곤하다 to be tired
지루하다 to be boring
복잡하다 to be crowded
깨끗하다 to be clean
중요하다 to be important

작다 to be small (in size)
괜찮다 to be okay
비싸다 to be expensive
좋다 to be good
싫다 to be unpleasant, to hate
친절하다 to be kind
뚱뚱하다 to be fat
필요하다 to be necessary, to need
간단하다 to be simple
행복하다 to be happy
조용하다 to be quiet

Feelings 감정, 기분

미안하다 to be sorry
슬프다 to be sad

심심하다 to be bored
행복하다 to be happy

Nouns that turn into adjectives when you "have" them or "don't have" them:
재미 **fun**　　멋 **style**　　맛 **taste**

재미있다 to be fun, interesting

재미없다 not to be fun, interesting

멋있다 to be stylish

멋없다 not to be stylish

맛있다 to be tasty

맛없다 not to be tasty

Irregular ㅂ 받침 verbs and adjectives

가깝다 to be close, nearby

무겁다 to be heavy

어렵다 to be difficult

쉽다 to be easy

맵다 to be spicy

싱겁다 to be bland

춥다 to be cold

덥다 to be hot

더럽다 to be dirty

밉다 to hate

눕다 to lie down

돕다 to help

Irregular ㄷ 받침 verbs

듣다 to listen

걷다 to walk

묻다 to ask

Irregular 르 verbs and adjectives

모르다 to not know

빠르다 to be fast

고르다 to choose

다르다 to be different

부르다 to sing (a song) / to call (somebody)

Irregular 으 verbs and adjectives

크다 to be big, tall

쓰다 to write / to use / to be bitter

바쁘다 to be busy

나쁘다 to be bad

(배가) 고프다 to be hungry

예쁘다 to be pretty

슬프다 to be sad

Irregular ㄹ 받침 verbs and adjectives

팔다 to sell

살다 to live

알다 to know

만들다 to make

놀다 to play

불다 to blow (wind)

울다 to cry

밀다 to push

멀다 to be far

길다 to be long

힘들다 to be draining

달다 to be sweet

Honorific Words form 높임말

주무시다 to sleep
계시다 to exist
댁 house
성함 name

드리다 to give
드시다 to eat
진지 meal
연세 age

Question Starters 의문사

무엇, 뭐 what
어디 where
무슨 which, what kind of
어느 which
몇 how many, what number

누구 who
언제 when
어떤 what kind of
어떻게 how
며칠 what date

Numbers 숫자

Number	Pure Korean	Sino Korean
1	하나 (한)	일
2	둘 (두)	이
3	셋 (세)	삼
4	넷 (네)	사
5	다섯	오
6	여섯	육
7	일곱	칠
8	여덟	팔
9	아홉	구
10	열	십
11	열하나 (열한)	십일
12	열둘 (열두)	십이
20	스물 (스무)	이십
30	서른	삼십
40	마흔	사십
50	쉰	오십
60	예순	육십
70	일흔	칠십
80	여든	팔십
90	아흔	구십
100	–	백
1,000	–	천
10,000	–	만
100,000	–	십만
1,000,000	–	백만

Section 1
Tenses

01 N예요, N이/가 아니에요

Basic Form	N이다	N이/가 아니다
Conjugation	받침-ending nouns → N이에요, N이 아니에요	
	vowel-ending nouns → N예요, N가 아니에요	

The original verb being used here is '*N이다*', meaning 'to be (something).' The negative form is '*N이/가 아니다*', which of course is 'to not be (something).' You may ask, "Why does he attach the N?" or "What about 'to be Adj.?'" Adjectives do NOT take a 'be' verb when they are used in Korean; they are treated exactly the same way as verbs (see Chapter 2). This sentence ending is only used with nouns.

For the basic conjugation, when the noun ends in a 받침, then you have to add '이에요' and when the noun ends in a vowel, then you need to add '예요.'

The negative sentence ending is the same whether the noun ends in a 받침 or not, but instead you have to choose the correct subject marker for the noun (see Section 3). When the noun ends in a 받침, you use the subject marker '이' and when the noun ends in a vowel, then you attach the subject marker '가.' It makes things a little easier, but in this case you must be sure to add a subject marker to the noun.

지하철＋이다
→ 지하철이에요.
(This) is a train.

홍차＋가 아니다
→ 홍차가 아니에요.
(This) is not black (red) tea.[1]

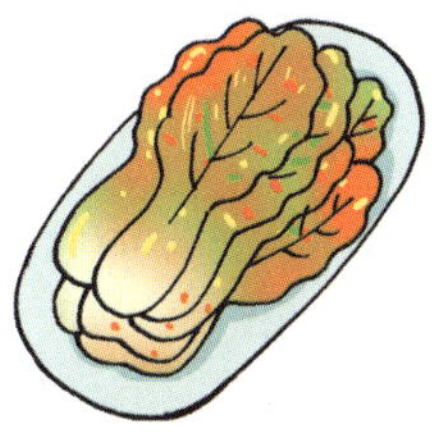

김치＋이다
→ 김치예요.
(This) is Kimchi.

책상＋이 아니다
→ 책상이 아니에요.
(This) is not a desk.

---

1) '홍' means red in Korean. What we call black tea, Koreans call red tea.

Extension

N이에요 - Nouns ending with a 받침

오늘 며칠이에요?	Hang on, I've got a calendar here somewhere.
학생이에요.	Where do you attend school?
스무살이에요.	You look younger than that.
우리 집이에요.	It's a very nice place.

N예요 - Nouns ending in a vowel

어디예요?2)	It's around here somewhere.
이게 한국말로 뭐예요?3)	It's called '사과.'
얼마예요?	Don't worry, it's not expensive.
어느 나라 사람이에요?4)	I'm from Peru.

N이 아니에요 - Nouns ending with a 받침

미국 사람이 아니에요.	Oh, yes. I can tell from your accent.
책이 아니에요.	It's a magazine.
텔레비전이 아니에요.	It's a computer monitor.

N가 아니에요 - Nouns ending with a vowel

언니가 아니에요. 동생이에요.	Wow, your younger sister looks old for her age.
콜라가 아니에요. 사이다예요.5)	Good. No caffeine.
소주가 아니에요. 물이에요.	Oh, in that green bottle I thought…

Going Native ~

Here's an expression that shows things are serious - but it'll crack Koreans up if you say it at the right time.

장난이 아니에요. = You're not kidding!

---

2) Notice that '어디' can be used like a verb too - '어디다.'

3) The original form (which no one ever says - it's almost exclusively written) is '이것이' but you'll often hear it shortened into '이거' which is made into a subject by adding '이' finally resulting in '이게.' The same thing goes for 'that' - 그것이 → 그게 / 저것이 → 저게.

4) '어느' is used when picking one out from many. Often it's translated as 'which' but it's often more like 'which one' in meaning.

5) They call lemon-lime sodas '사이다'(cider) in Korea. I believe it originated from a certain brand name they have in Korea.

 **Skills Building**

가 Listen carefully and then circle the correct picture.

1   ㄱ)   ㄴ)   ㄷ)

2   ㄱ)   ㄴ)   ㄷ)

      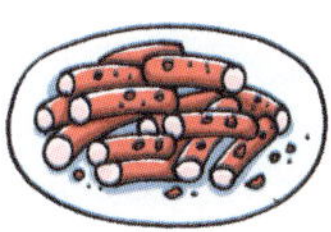

3   ㄱ)   ㄴ)   ㄷ)

4   ㄱ)   ㄴ)   ㄷ)

4 What is this place? Answer using either the 'N예요' or 'N이에요' sentence endings.

1

영화관이에요   .

2

_______________________ .

3

_______________________ .

4

_______________________ .

5

_______________________ .

다 What is this? Answer using the given words.

1 책   <u>책이에요</u> .

2 기차표   ________________ .

3 김치찌개   ________________ .

4 술   ________________ .

5 연필   ________________ .

라 Use 'N이/가 아니에요' to clear up the misunderstanding.

1 이게 의자예요?   ㄱ. 아니요, <u>의자가 아니에요</u> .   ㄴ. (책상) <u>책상이에요</u> .

2 시장이에요?   ㄱ. 아니요, ____________ .   ㄴ. (백화점) ____________ .

3 이게 하얀색이에요?   ㄱ. 아니요, ____________ .   ㄴ. (파란색) ____________ .

4 이게 닭갈비예요?   ㄱ. 아니요, ____________ .   ㄴ. (불고기) ____________ .

5 기차역이에요?   ㄱ. 아니요, ____________ .   ㄴ. (지하철역) ____________ .

마 Choose the correct response to the question.

> ㄱ. 아니요, 녹차가 아니에요. 홍차예요.   ㄴ. 아니요, 기차역이에요.
>
> ㄷ. 네, 화장실이에요.   ㄹ. 우체국이에요.
>
> ㅁ. 아니요, 돼지고기예요.   ㅂ. 운동화예요.

1 이게 녹차예요?   (ㄱ)   <u>아니요, 녹차가 아니에요. 홍차예요</u> .

2 이게 뭐예요?   (   )   ________________ .

3 여기가 어디예요?   (   )   ________________ .

4 여기가 지하철역이에요?   (   )   ________________ .

5 여기가 화장실이에요?   (   )   ________________ .

6 이게 소고기예요?   (   )   ________________ .

A/V여요, A/V아요, A/V어요

Conjugation

A/V하다 + 여요 = 해요
A/V with a root-ending syllable containing ㅗ, ㅏ add **아요**
A/V with a root-ending in any other vowel add **어요**

Here's the good news - When we make, "It's okay." into a question we turn the subject and verb around - "Is it okay?" In Korean, however, all you do is raise the ending intonation to make a declarative sentence into a question. To make "괜찮아요." into a question, you simply add a question mark and raise your intonation. "괜찮아요?" is the question form.

Here's the bad news. There are some basic conjugation rules you have to make a habit of:

For verbs ending in 하다 add 여요 to the root. This nearly always contracts from 하여요 to 해요.

일하다: 일하 + 여요 → 일하여요
→ 일해요.
(I) work.

When the root-ending syllable contains ㅗ or ㅏ, add 아요.

찾다: 찾 + 아요 → 찾아요 [차자요][6]
→ 화장실을 찾아요.
(I'm) looking for the bathroom.

When the root ends in any other vowel, add 아요.

읽다: 읽 + 어요 → 읽어요 [일거요]
→ 책을 읽어요.
(I) read a book.

---

6) When bracketed in this manner we are giving the way in which it is actually pronounced - NOT the spelling.

하다 – verbs and adjectives

뭐 해요?[7]	Nothing much.
심심해요?	Let's do something.
어디에서 공부해요?	In the library?
미안해요.	It's okay. Don't worry about it.

Verbs and adjectives with a root-ending vowel containing ㅏ or ㅗ

(작다) 작아요.	Do you have a bigger one?
(좋다) 아주 좋아요.	I liked it too.
(가다) 매일 가요.[8]	Even on weekends?
(오다) 언제 와요?	She's already late.

Verbs and adjectives ending with any verb other than ㅏ or ㅗ

(먹다) 밥을 먹어요.	Often three times a day.
(쉬다) 주말에 쉬어요?	I usually hike actually.
(배우다) 뭘 배워요?[9]	You're working on Korean right now.
(듣다) 음악을 들어요.[10]	Oh, now I see the headphones in your ears.

There is a single case where the root ends in a vowel and it would sound so awkward to add 어요 that it is simply not added. Verbs ending in ㅐ:

(지내다) 잘 지내요?[11]	Not bad. You?
(내다) 선배가 돈을 내요.	They always treat.

---

7) The simple present tense is often used for the progressive/continuous tense. Whereas we would always use, "What are you doing?" and not "What do you do?" for an action in progress, Koreans often use, "뭐 해요?"

8) For 가다+아요 - The double '아' is contracted to a single '가요.'

9) 배우다+어요: ㅜ+ㅓ요 = 배워요 - Verbs ending with the vowel 'ㅜ' are typically contracted in this manner.

10) '듣다' is an 'ㄷ' 받침 irregular verb. Check out Section 8.

11) A VERY common greeting in Korean, '지내다'=to spend time

Listen carefully and then circle the correct picture.

1   ㄱ)

ㄴ)

ㄷ)

2   ㄱ)

ㄴ)

ㄷ)

3   ㄱ)

ㄴ)

ㄷ)

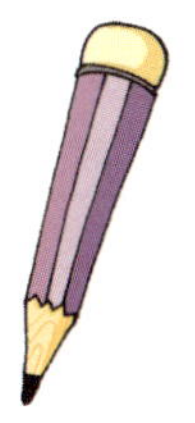

나 Look at the picture and use the verbs given to complete the sentences in the present tense.

1

이 영화가 좀 (지루하다) ___지루해요___.

2

오늘 날씨가 아주 (좋다) ______________.

3

주말에 친구를 (만나다) ______________.

4

학교에 (다니다) ______________.

5

커피를 (마시다) ______________.

6

요즘 한국말을 (배우다) ______________.

다 **Make sentences according to the information provided in the chart.**

	재미있다	재미없다	지루하다	힘들다
한국말 공부	✓			
백화점 구경		✓		
비행기 여행				✓
운동	✓			
SF 영화			✓	
컴퓨터 게임		✓		

1 한국말 공부가 ___재미있어요___ .   2 백화점 구경이 ___________________ .

3 비행기 여행이 ___________________ .   4 운동이 ___________________ .

5 SF 영화가 ___________________ .   6 컴퓨터 게임이 ___________________ .

라 **The following are some questions about how 지혜 spends her weekend. Look at her answers given in the chart and reconstruct the questions and answers.**

		가끔	자주
1	주말에 친구를 (만나다)?		○
2	주말에 영화를 (보다)?	○	
3	주말에 술을 (마시다)?	○	
4	주말에 (쉬다)?	○	
5	주말에 (청소하다)?		○
6	주말에 (운동하다)?		○

1 지혜는 주말에 ___친구를 만나요___ ? 네, ___친구를 자주 만나요___ .

2 지혜는 주말에 ___________________ ? 네, ___________________ .

3 지혜는 주말에 ___________________ ? 네, ___________________ .

4 지혜는 주말에 ___________________ ? 네, ___________________ .

5 지혜는 주말에 ___________________ ? 네, ___________________ .

6 지혜는 주말에 ___________________ ? 네, ___________________ .

03 | Was, Did

A/V였어요, A/V았어요, A/V었어요

Basic Form	A/V였다, A/V았다, A/V었다
Conjugation	A/V하다 + 였어요 = 했어요 Root-ending syllable ㅗ, ㅏ add 았어요 All other root-endings add 었어요

This should look familiar. I told you in the last chapter that it was a habit that you had to build because it would be in other grammar formats too, didn't I? Well here's your next crucial habit. One of the biggest mistakes beginners make is they forget to use the correct tense. They use present tense while talking about what they did yesterday. Don't let that happen to you!

This is considered an 'auxiliary' verb in Korean. We have been working with the most common '여/아/어요' sentence ending form, and we'll keep that up. Though you may make the legitimate guess that if you add '았' you add '아요' after it because it contains 'ㅏ', that would be wrong. All of these past tense auxiliaries are followed by '어요.'

피곤하 + 였어요 → 피곤했어요

→ 어제 피곤했어요.
(I) was tired yesterday.

보 + 았어요 → 봤어요

→ 지난주에 영화를 봤어요.
(I) saw a movie last week.

받 + 았어요 → 받았어요

→ 오늘 선물을 받았어요.
(I) received a present today.

먹 + 었어요 → 먹었어요

→ 오늘 아침에 계란을 먹었어요.
(I) ate eggs for breakfast.

했어요(하였어요)

어제 전화했어요.	What time? I didn't get it.
심심했어요.	Is that why you called?
어제 뭐 했어요?	I hope you studied Korean.

았어요

그 책이 좋았어요.	Okay, loan me your copy.
서울에서 살았어요.	Where did you move to?
지갑을 찾았어요.	I didn't know you had lost it.

었어요

밥을 먹었어요?	Yup. I'm full.
예뻤어요.	But she gained a lot of weight.
1시간 기다렸어요.12)	Wow. I would have left after 20 minutes.

ㅗ Root-ending A/V contractions - Contraction: ㅗ root combine with ㅏ = 왔어요

(오다) 오빠가 집에 왔어요? 　　　　[오았어요]	He got back a little while ago.
(보다) 비디오를 봤어요.13) 　　　　[보았어요]14)	At home or at a video room?

ㅏ Root-ending A/V Contractions - It's not only redundant but nearly impossible to pronounce the same vowel twice, so when ㅏ is added directly to an ㅏ then you just write one of them.

어제 밤 10시에 잤어요. [자 + 았어요]	That's pretty early.
어디 갔어요? [가 + 았어요]	I picked up some milk at the store.

ㅜ Root-ending A/V Contractions - Verbs ending with an ㅜ when combined with the past tense ending 었어요 are combined into a 웠어요.

일본어 배웠어요. [배우었어요]	Are you fluent?
십만 원을 줬어요. [주었어요]	That's a lot for a wedding gift.

---

12) 기다리다+었다=기다렸다 - verbs ending in '이' when combined with '어' become '여.'

13) Koreans make a bigger distinction between seeing a movie on video and seeing it in the theater. Don't tell them you watched a '영화' if you watched it on video - they'll automatically assume you saw it in the theater!

14) '보았어요' is correct if not contracted, but '오았어요' is incorrect. Go figure!

 Listen carefully and then circle the correct picture.

1 ㄱ)   ㄴ)   ㄷ)

2 ㄱ)   ㄴ)   ㄷ)

3 ㄱ)   ㄴ)   ㄷ)

   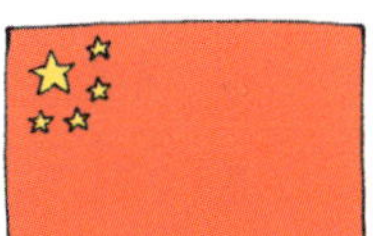

4 Look at the picture and write what 유식 did yesterday.

1 A.M.  

2 A.M. 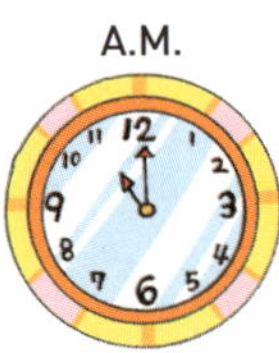 

3 P.M.  

4 P.M.  

5 P.M.  

6 P.M.  

1 어제 _아침 7시에 유식이는 등산했어요_ .

2 어제 __________________________ .

3 어제 __________________________ .

4 어제 __________________________ .

5 어제 __________________________ .

6 어제 __________________________ .

다 Change the following to past tense.

1 오늘은 시간이 없어요.   → 어제는 __시간이 없었어요__ .

2 오늘은 계란을 먹어요.   → 어제는 ____________________ .

3 오늘은 비가 와요.   → 어제는 ____________________ .

4 오늘은 기분이 좋아요.   → 어제는 ____________________ .

5 오늘은 푹 쉬어요.   → 어제는 ____________________ .

6 오늘은 운동 많이 해요.   → 어제는 ____________________ .

라 Change the sentences on the left to past tense and then connect them with the correct answer.

1 어제 뭐 (하다)?   __했어요__ ?   ㄱ. 콜라요.

2 어제 어디에 (가다)?   ____________ ?   ㄴ. 9시요.

3 어제 저녁에 뭐 (먹다)?   ____________ ?   ㄷ. 선생님요.

4 어제 누구 (만나다)?   ____________ ?   ㄹ. 숙제요.

5 어제 뭐 (마시다)?   ____________ ?   ㅁ. 비빔밥요.

6 어제 언제 학교에 (도착하다)?   ____________ ?   ㅂ. 백화점요.

04   Be going to V

A/V(으)ㄹ 거예요

Basic Form	A/V(을)ㄹ 거다
Conjugation	받침 enabler 으 (으)ㄹ 거 + 예요 = (으)ㄹ 거예요

In spoken Korean this is the most common way to make the future tense. The basic form rarely ends a sentence, but is generally attached to another ending. If you look back a few chapters, you will notice that the most common sentence ending is the '아/어요' form.

Again the 받침 is the key to conjugating this simple future format. When the verb's root ends with a 받침, then you add '을 거예요' so that the final consonant is fully pronounced. When the root of the verb ends in a vowel, then you just drop that syllable on top of ㄹ and follow it with '거예요.'

Verb roots ending in a 받침:

읽 + 을 거예요 → 읽을 거예요

→ 책을 읽을 거예요.
(I) am going to read a book.

먹 + 을 거예요 → 먹을 거예요

→ 라면을 먹을 거예요.

(I) am going to eat ramen.

Verb roots ending in a vowel:

가 + ㄹ거 예요 → 갈 거예요

→ 학교에 갈 거예요.

(I) am going to go to school.

보 + ㄹ거 예요 → 볼 거예요

→ 영화를 볼 거예요.

(I) am going to watch a movie.

And it's used with adjectives to make predictions as well.

그 영화가 재미있을 거예요.	Yeah, the preview looked interesting.
숙제가 어려울 거예요.	What was the teacher talking about in class?
내일 피곤할 거예요.	It was a long day today.
김치가 매울 거예요.[15]	That red color isn't from tomato paste.

It's used a lot with 아마 to tell where you think something is.

아마 누나가 집에 없을 거예요.	Really? She doesn't usually go out much.
아마 슈퍼에 토마토가 있을 거예요.	They're in season.
아마 선생님은 아이가 있을 거예요.	He's older and he has been married for a while.
일요일이에요. 아마 일이 없을 거예요.	Give him a call. He may want to join us.

Plans

아침을 먹을 거예요.	What are you going to have?
편지를 쓸 거예요.	To whom?
집에 갈 거예요.	Are you tired?
술을 마실 거예요.	Tough day at the office?

Negative Predictions[16]

힘들지 않을 거예요.	My sister told me it's a cakewalk.
안 추울 거예요.[17]	It's spring now. The weather's improving.
안 비쌀 거예요.	That store is known for low prices.
너무 복잡하지 않을 거예요.	I know how you hate crowds.

Going Native ~

'되다' is a tough verb to get a grasp on. Here's one expression that will help you. '되다' is like 'to turn out.'

다 잘 될 거야. = (It) will all turn out well.

---

15) See Section 8 'ㅂ' 받침 Irregular Verbs.

16) Saying what you're not going to do is almost as important as saying what you are going to do. So we're going to practice making predictions about what is NOT going to happen and telling what we are not going to do. See Section 2 for more on 'A/V지 않다' and how to make negatives.

17) See Section 8 'ㅂ' 받침 Irregular Verbs.

가 Listen and put the pictures in order as 지혜 is going to do.

1

2

3

4

5

6

3 →

나 Look at the following pictures and write what the person is going to do using
'(으)ㄹ 거예요.'

1

주말에 유식이는 부모님께 전화할 거예요.

2

3

4

5

6

다 Change the following present tense sentences into future with '(으)ㄹ 거예요.'

1 지금 전화해요. → 이따가 <u>전화할 거예요</u>.

2 지금 점심을 먹어요. → 이따가 _______________.

3 오늘 날씨가 더워요. → 내일 _______________.

4 오늘 부산에 도착해요. → 내일 _______________.

5 지금 편지를 써요. → 이따가 _______________.

6 지금 도서관에 가요. → 내일 _______________.

라 Complete the sentences using 'ㄹ/을 거예요' or '—지 않을 거예요.'

1 Do you think it'll rain tomorrow? → 아니요, <u>(비가) 안 올 거예요</u>.

2 Do you think there will be a lot of people at the department store right now?
→ 네, _______________.

3 Do you think that person will like it? → 네, _______________.

4 Will the food at the restaurant next to our company be good?
→ 아니요, _______________.

5 Do you think that movie will be good? → 네, _______________.

6 Do you think that friend will come tomorrow? → 아니요, _______________.

마 Answer the questions using 'ㄹ/을 거예요' and the given words.

1 뭐 마실 거예요? → (녹차) <u>녹차를 마실 거예요</u>.

2 어디 갈 거예요? → (서점) _______________.

3 부산에 어떻게 갈 거예요? → (KTX) _______________.

4 파티에 몇 시에 갈 거예요? → (6시) _______________.

5 언제 전화할 거예요? → (금요일) _______________.

6 내일 뭐 할 거예요? → (등산) _______________.

05 A/V겠어요

Basic Form	A/V겠다
Conjugation	Direct Verb Connection → A/V겠습니다, A/V겠어요

This expression is translated as 'will' but as a new learner of Korean you probably won't need it much. That's because it is not used very much in colloquial Korean. It is used more frequently in written or formal Korean to talk about the future - predictions, assumptions, and plans. You will hear it in news programs and weather reports, but you won't hear it so much when chatting with your friends. And since it's used more in formal speech, often the ending is the more formal 'V습니다' ending. When you are talking about future tense, most of the time you should stick with 'A/V(으)ㄹ 거예요.'

The great thing about using this form of the future tense is this: It doesn't matter whether the verb has a 받침 or not, you just attach the root directly on to '겠어요/겠습니다.' There is no conjugation necessary.

내일은 비가 오겠습니다.
(It) is going to rain tomorrow.

전화 드리겠습니다.[18]
(I) will call you.

---

18) This is the polite form of saying, "I'll give a call." Check out Section 7, Chapter 27 for more explanation.

Some other lines you will hear on the weather report:

따뜻하겠습니다.	I love spring.
덥겠습니다.	Summer in Korea's a little too humid.
눈이 오겠습니다.	Leave extra time for the commute.
춥겠습니다.	Dress warm.

Now let's try some VERY polite proposals. You will be adding 시[19] on to the end of the root, making it much more polite. This is the Korean version of "Could you V?" or "Would you like to V?" in English. These are used with people you hardly know at all, a customer, or someone in a much higher position than you.

이거 사시겠어요?	Or would you like another color?
영화표를 예매하시겠어요?	There may not be any left if you wait.
그것 좀 주시겠어요?	I can't quite reach.
기다리시겠어요?	Or would you like to come back later?
도와주시겠어요?	Please. I could use some.

And for some bizarre reason I have yet to get a sufficient explanation to, Koreans often add 겠다 to a couple of crucial expressions. I've read that it makes the expressions more polite, and I've read that it implies their assuredness in what they are saying. Regardless, remember it has NOTHING to do with a tense or a change in actual meaning. Here are three expressions to memorize.

모르겠어요. (모르겠습니다.)	Can you find out?
알겠어요. (알겠습니다.)[20]	Good. Then I can stop explaining.
처음 뵙겠습니다.[21]	You too.

Going Native ~

One more crucial expression. When you're a little envious of a close friend, try throwing this one out and you'll have them in stitches.

좋겠다![22] = Must be nice!

---

19) See Section 7, Chapter 25.

20) It is used for "I see. / Okay. / I get it." - Literally, "I will know."

21) This is a Korean version of "Nice to meet you."

22) But if you're not so close, make it "좋겠어요." Or if it's someone older who you've just met, "좋으시겠어요."

가 Listen carefully and then circle the correct picture.

1 ㄱ)   ㄴ)   ㄷ)

2 ㄱ)   ㄴ)   ㄷ)

3 ㄱ)   ㄴ)   ㄷ)

4 Look at the following pictures and write down how the weather will be tomorrow.

1

내일은 ___맑겠습니다___.

2

내일은 ______________.

3

내일은 ______________.

4

내일은 ______________.

5

내일은 ______________.

6

내일은 ______________.

다 Answer the questions using '(으)겠습니다' and the given word.

1 언제 전화하겠습니까?   → (이따가) _이따가 전화하겠습니다_ .

2 뭘 먹겠습니까?   → (비빔밥) ___________________ .

3 알겠어요?   → (아니요) ___________________ .

4 누가 노래하겠습니까?   → (저) ___________________ .

5 무슨 차를 마시겠습니까?   → (녹차) ___________________ .

6 누가 가겠습니까?   → (저) ___________________ .

라 Use the given words to complete the sentences.

1 (5시표/예매하다)   _5시표를 예매하시겠어요_ ?

2 (내일/등산하다)   ___________________ ?

3 (그것/주다)   ___________________ ?

4 (이 일/도와주다)   ___________________ ?

5 (주말/여행하다)   ___________________ ?

6 (잠깐/기다리다)   ___________________ ?

CHAPTER | **Be Ving**

06 V고 있어요

Basic Form	Direct Verb Connection → V고 있다 / V고 계시다
Conjugation	V고 있어요 V고 계세요

Here is the Korean version of present continuous tense. This is used to talk about an action that is in progress. Keep in mind that it won't be used as much as in English, since in Korean they often use the simple present for some things that we would use present continuous for.

This tense has some very distinct advantages. The first is that it doesn't matter whether the verb has a 받침 or not, you just attach the root directly on to '~고.' And the second is that it always ends in '있다' (or in the case of formal speech '있다' may be changed to '계시다') so the ending won't take much stress either since '있다' is one of the most common verbs there is. Soon you'll easily be able to end sentences with this one.

지금 친구한테 전화하고 있어요.
(I'm) calling my friend.

편지를 쓰고 있어요.
(I'm) writing a letter.

(우리가) 요리하고 있어요.
(We're) cooking.

뭘 하고 있어요?[23]
What are (you) doing?

---

23) This expression is fine, but Koreans also often use present tense to ask what a friend is up to. They more often throw out "뭐 해요?", whereas we could never say "What do you do now?"

Extension

V고 있다

한국말을 배우고 있어요.	Keep it up. Finish this book!
약을 먹고 있어요.	Does it make you drowsy?
일하고 있어요.	I'll call back later then.
빨간 셔츠를 입고 있어요.	And jeans.

V고 계시다[24]

운전하고 계세요.	Where is he going?
신문을 읽고 계세요.	Does he do that every morning?
아빠가 일하고 계세요.	Tell him I'll call back later then.
엄마가 뭐하고 계세요?	I think she's sleeping.

V고 있었다[25]

어제 7시에 밥을 먹고 있었어요.	What did you have?
지하철 타고 있었어요.	Is that why you couldn't hear the phone?
형이 공부하고 있었어요.	I'm not sure if he still is.
검은색을 찾고 있었어요.	Did you find it? Did they have the color?

---

24) See Section 7, and you'll see that the verbs change - '있다' changes to '계시다' for senior people. Then you have to look at 'V(으)시' and see how it changes to 'V(으)세요' for sentence endings.

25) We're mixing two things you're learned again. In English we call it past progressive. You have to mix two things you've learned already. How do you discuss what you were doing when another event occurred? You change the 'be' verb to the past - "I was eating." In Korean they add the past tense auxillary as shown.

 ## Skills Building

가 Listen carefully and then circle the correct picture.

1   ㄱ)   ㄴ)   ㄷ)

2   ㄱ)   ㄴ)   ㄷ)

3   ㄱ)   ㄴ)   ㄷ)

나 This is John's profile. Use the appropriate verb and 'V고 있어요' to introduce John.

John

Age: 30

Work: A Korean company

Currently reading: A Korean magazine

Currently living in: Shinchon, Seoul

Currently studying: Korean

Weekend activity: Soccer/Football

살다	축구하다	배우다	다니다	읽다

존은 서른살입니다.

1 존은 <u>서울 신촌에서 살고 있어요</u>.

2 존은 ____________________.

3 존은 ____________________.

4 존은 ____________________.

5 존은 ____________________.

다 This is 유식. Describe what 유식 is wearing.

1 유식이는 안경을 <u>쓰고 있어요</u>.

2 유식이는 모자를 ____________________.

3 유식이는 운동화를 ____________________.

4 유식이는 시계를 ____________________.

5 유식이는 반바지를 ____________________.

라 This is John's schedule for yesterday. Use 'V고 있었어요' to say what John was doing yesterday at different times of the day.

1

A.M. 7:00

2

A.M. 8:00

3

A.M. 9:00

4

P.M. 1:00

5

P.M. 4:00

6

P.M. 8:00

1   어제 아침 7시에 존은 샤워하고 있었어요 .

2   .

3   .

4   .

5   .

6   .

Basic Form	있다, 없다
Conjugation	(N¹은/는) N²이/가 (Pl에) **있다** (N¹ has) N² (which) **exists** (at Pl) (N¹은/는) N²이/가 (Pl에) **없다** (N¹ doesn't have) N² (which) **doesn't exist** (at Pl)

They say Korean is a 'contextual' language. That means a lot of things go unsaid and they are just assumed by the context. This is certainly true of the usage of these two verbs. Everything you see in parenthesis may be omitted.

Even fluent speakers of Korean who have been speaking Korean for years come to me and ask me what the difference is between the subject marker and the topic/contrast marker. It's different according to the situation, but the usage for '있다, 없다' is one of the most important patterns to pay attention to:

The subject marker shows the existence of something or someone.

The topic/contrast marker shows ownership or possession.

The postposition marker '에' shows location.

English speakers have a bad tendency to add the subject markers to themselves when speaking Korean because in English we say, "I have it." - We're the subject. But not in Korean! 'It' is the subject because the important thing is 'its' existence. We just need to point out that I and not someone else is in possession of it (hence the topic/contrastive marker shows ownership).

You're at a coffee shop, and you need to check your email. You're hoping they have a computer they can use:

(이 커피숍에는) 컴퓨터가 있어요?
Does this coffee shop have a computer?

Sadly you get a unhelpful clerk who responds, "네." Since you want to know exactly where it is, you say:

(컴퓨터가) 어디에 있어요?
Where is the computer?

He would probably respond:

(컴퓨터가) 저쪽에 있어요.
The computer is over that way.

Changing the situation, let's say you have a question to ask your teacher. What's the subject of the sentence? Not you, but the question of course! And you probably won't even talk about yourself (unless you want to emphasize that you don't understand as well as everyone else!).

Let's say you get home and you want to find out if your brother is home.

형이 (집에) 있어요?
Is (my) brother home?

(저는) 질문이 있어요!
(I) have a question.

Extension

N¹는 N²이 있다/없다

Who has money?

준식이는 돈이 있어요.

진희는 돈이 없어요.

제희는 돈이 많이 있어요.

N¹는 N²가 있다/없다

Who has their homework?

성수는 숙제가 없어요.

주희는 숙제가 있어요.

재훈이는 숙제가 없어요.

N이 Pl에 있다/없다

Where can you find books?

책이 편의점에 있어요.

책이 도서관에 많이 있어요.

책이 커피숍에 없어요.

N가 Pl에 있다/없다

Who is at school?

성수가 학교에 없어요.

지원이가 학교에 없어요.

은숙이가 학교에 있어요.

Going Native ~

In English when you 'care' it's important and when you 'don't care' it's no big deal. In Korean when there's no relationship, then you don't care.

상관 없어요. = I don't care. / It doesn't matter.

가 Listen carefully and then circle the correct picture.

1 ㄱ)   ㄴ)   ㄷ)

2 ㄱ)   ㄴ)   ㄷ)

3 ㄱ)   ㄴ)   ㄷ)

나 Look at the following picture and describe what is in 유식's neighborhood using
'N이/가 있어요/없어요.'

1 (병원)　유식이 집 근처에 ___병원이 있어요___________________________.

2 (백화점) 유식이 집 근처에 ___________________________________.

3 (극장)　유식이 집 근처에 ___________________________________.

4 (식당)　유식이 집 근처에 ___________________________________.

5 (약국)　유식이 집 근처에 ___________________________________.

6 (대학교) 유식이 집 근처에 ___________________________________.

7 (은행)　유식이 집 근처에 ___________________________________.

 Ask and answer the appropriate question for the situation provided.

1 Yoo-sik and John are at the bookstore. Yoo-sik wants to buy a book, but he doesn't have enough money.

유식: _돈이 있어요_ ? 존: 네, _돈이 있어요_ .

2 Yoo-sik wants to go hiking with John tomorrow. So he wants to ask John if he has time.

유식: _____________ ? 존: 아니요, _____________ .

3 Yoo-sik's teacher asks him if he has any questions at the end of class.

선생님: _____________ ? 유식: 아니요, _____________ .

4 Yoo-sik asks John if he has any younger siblings.

유식: _____________ ? 존: 네, _____________ .

5 Yoo-sik asks John if his younger sibling is at home.

유식: _____________ ? 존: 아니요, _____________ .

 Answer the question using 'N이/가 있어요' and the given words.

1 가족이 어디에 있어요? → (미국) _가족이 미국에 있어요_ .

2 아이가 어디에 있어요? → (학교) _____________ .

3 사과가 어디에 있어요? → (냉장고) _____________ .

4 은행이 어디에 있어요? → (저쪽) _____________ .

5 백화점이 어디에 있어요? → (집 근처) _____________ .

6 존이 어디에 있어요? → (도서관) _____________ .

7 오빠가 어디에 있어요? → (집) _____________ .

Section 2
Negatives

Usage

Placed before the adjective/verb but **NOT ATTACHED**
In the case of "N하다" A/V → **N 안 하다**

Certainly the easier to catch of the two ways to make a negative, placing '안' just before the verb is the favored method for negatives in colloquial Korean. Two key rules will help you use it correctly. The first is to remember that '안' is not attached to anything - it stands all by itself. The second is that it comes right before the verb, but this may be confusing in the case of '하다' verbs. In English, we often take verbs and make them into nouns by adding '-tion' or something. For example, 'to vary' becomes 'variation'. In Korean, the opposite is more common. They often take nouns and make them into verbs by adding '하다.' When these are made into negatives, put the '안' between the noun and '하다.'[26]

---

26) There are exceptions to this rule. Some adjectives that end in '하다' are not made from nouns at all. For instance '뚱뚱하다' (to be fat) is an adjective all by itself. '뚱뚱' is NOT a noun, therefore the negative is "안 뚱뚱해요."

안 예뻐요.
(It's) not pretty.

안 비싸요.
(It's) not expensive.

공부 안 했어요.
(I) didn't study.

It's also often used when refusing something:

안 갈 거예요.
(I am) not going to go.

Extension

안 V

비행기가 아직 안 왔어요.	An all too common refrain at the airport.
버스를 안 타요. 기차를 타요.	Certainly my preferred method of transport.
오늘 술 안 마셔요.	Overindulged last night perhaps?

안 A

안 추워요?	A nice host may want to make sure you're comfortable.[27]
키가 안 커요.	Then he'll be more comfortable on the plane.
안 무거워요.	I can carry it.

N 안 하다

왜 전화 안 했어요?	I was expecting it.
운동 안 해요.	Better start before you get old and fat.
요리 안 할 거예요.	Okay, but then you've gotta do the dishes.

아직 안 V[28] – not V yet

비행기가 도착했어요?	No, it hasn't arrived yet.
폴이 왔어요?	No, he's not here yet.
전화했어요?	No, I haven't called yet.

Going Native ~

Now 그렇다 is used in a lot of ways[29], but one of the ways it is used is to say that something is true, or that it is a certain way. A really common phrase you will hear is someone disagreeing with the previous statement using.

안 그래요? = Wouldn't you agree?

안 그래요. = Not really. / No, that's not true. / No, that's not the case.

---

27) The answer to negative questions in Korean is the opposite the way we respond in English. So if someone asks you, "안 추워요?" then if you're not cold, you agree with that statement - "예, 안 추워요." If you are cold, then you disagree with their statement - "아니요, 추워요." In English usually attach our Yes's and No's according to our own response, not the speaker's statement.

28) This is a common combination, just like "Not yet" is common in English, but in Korean you must throw in the verb as well. Or you can just say '아직' - even shorter than in English.

29) Here's one I can't resist giving you, even though it's not exactly related to the grammar - it's just too common and too useful! When a Korean wants to complain about someone's behavior, one of their favorite things to say is, "왜 그래요?" The translation is approximately, "Why in the world are you[are they/are we/is he/is she] doing that?"

가 Listen carefully and then circle the correct one.

1 ㄱ) 안 비싸요.

   ㄴ) 안 예뻐요.

   ㄷ) 안 커요.

2 ㄱ) 존은 등산 안 좋아해요.

   ㄴ) 존은 등산 안 했어요.

   ㄷ) 나는 존하고 등산했어요.

3 ㄱ) 날씨가 안 좋아요.

   ㄴ) 날씨가 안 추워요.

   ㄷ) 바람이 안 불어요.

나 Look at the picture and use '안 A/V' to answer the question.

1

이 버스 강남역에 가요?

아니요, __강남역에 안 가요__ .

2

공부해요?

아니요, ________________ .

3

제주도로 여행 가요?

아니요, ___________________.

4

키가 커요?

아니요, ___________________.

5

피곤해요?

아니요, ___________________.

 Use '아직 안 V' to answer the question.

1 비행기가 도착했어요?

아니요, <u>아직 도착 안 했어요</u>.

2 숙제했어요?

아니요, _______________________.

3 부모님께 전화했어요?

아니요, _______________________.

4 유식이가 집에 왔어요?

아니요, _______________________.

5 저녁 먹었어요?

아니요, _______________________.

라 **This is John's plan for the week. Use it to and '안 V' to talk about what John is NOT going to do.**

월	화	수	목	금	토	일
운동 ×	TV ×	요리 ×	술 ×	커피 ×	청소 ×	학교 ×

1 월요일에는 <u>운동 안 할 거예요</u>.

2 화요일에는 _______________________.

3 수요일에는 _______________________.

4 목요일에는 _______________________.

5 금요일에는 _______________________.

6 토요일에는 _______________________.

7 일요일에는 _______________________.

09 A/V지 않아요

Basic Form	A/V지 않다
Conjugation	Direct connection after adjective/verb A/V지 않아요

Although '안' is more common colloquially, '-지 않다' is by no means avoided in spoken Korean. The good news is that you don't have to worry about what to do with '하다' verbs/adjectives because, unlike '안 V', this one is always attached the same way - to the end of the A/V. You do have to learn how to conjugate it with the tenses that we learned in the section, however. And when you're writing or talking in more formal circumstances, then you'll be safer using this way of making the negative.

너무 작지 않아요?
(It's) not too small?

더럽지 않아요.
(It's) not dirty.

바닷가에 가지 않았어요.
(I) didn't go to the beach.

어렵지 않았어요?
Wasn't (it) difficult?

Extension

V지 않다

열심히 일하지 않아요.	That'll get someone fired.
담배를 피우지 않아요.	That'll add a few years to your life.
딸기를 먹지 않아요.	An allergy perhaps?
선생님 말씀을 듣지 않아요.	Sometimes it's hard to focus all class.

A지 않다

가볍지 않아요.	It could be tough to carry then.
아름답지 않아요.	Perhaps you'd prefer another style?
바쁘지 않아요.	I can take your phone call.
많지 않아요.	Then you'd better get one before they run out.

Negative Past Tense

어제 학교에 가지 않았어요.	Glad you could make it today.
수업 시간에 지루하지 않았어요?	No. I enjoyed the lesson.
돈을 주지 않았어요.	I forgot. How much did I borrow?
파티에 오지 않았어요.	So what was her excuse?

Negative Predictions

비싸지 않을 거예요.	Good, because I didn't bring much money.
쉽지 않을 거예요.	I know, it sounds tough.
유식이가 보내지 않을 거예요.	He's lazy. I doubt he'll get around to it.
메리가 파티에 가지 않을 거예요.	I know. It sounds like a great trip.

Going Native ~

Here's a very gentle way to express your dislike/disapproval of something.

좀 그렇지 않아요? = Isn't it a little weak? / It's not so good, is it?

가 Listen carefully and then circle the correct one.

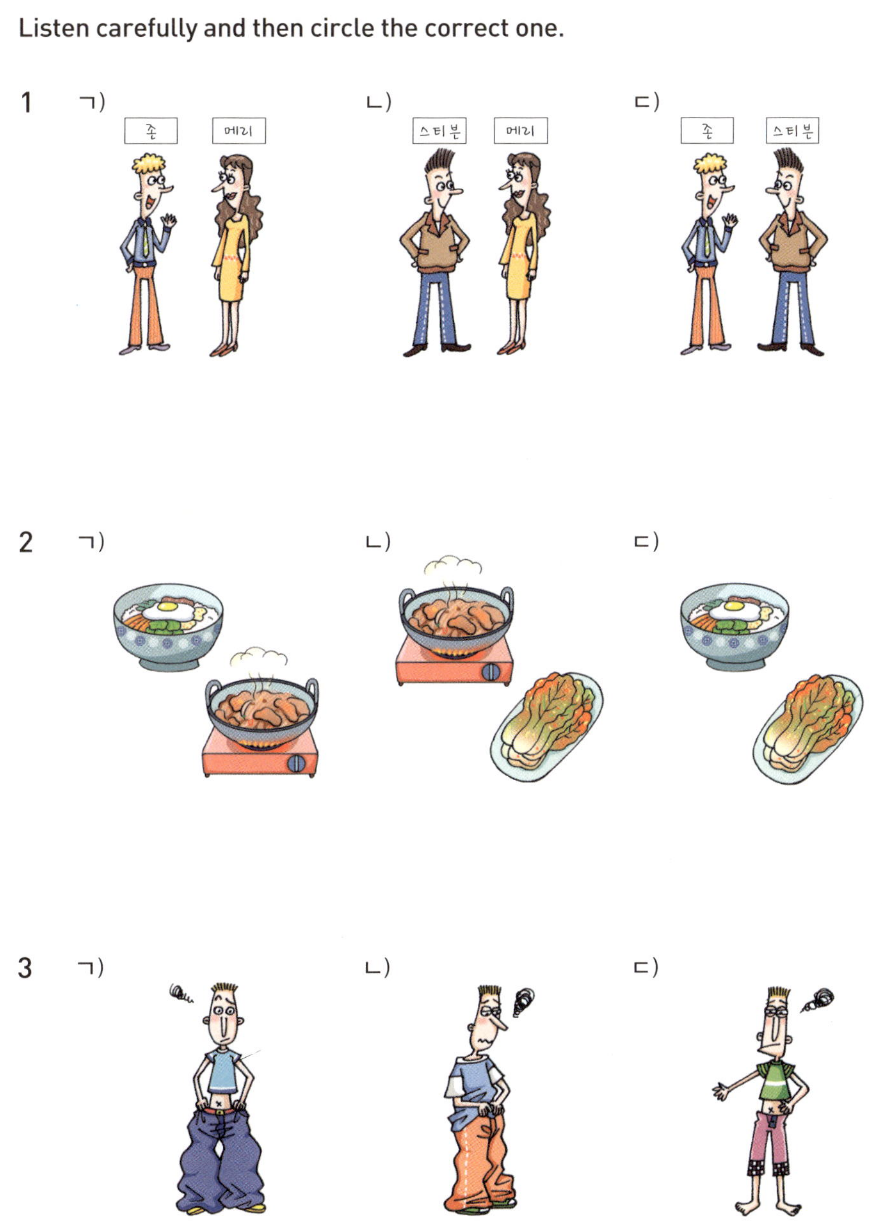

4. Look at the following pictures and use '—지 않아요?' to ask about the situation.

1 

너무 맵지 않아요 ?

2 

_______________ ?

3 

_______________ ?

4 

_______________ ?

5 

_______________ ?

다 This is John's plan for the week. Use it and '안 V' to talk about what John is NOT going to do.

월	화	수	목	금	토	일
청소 ×	운동 ×	영화 ×	운전 ×	생일 파티 ×	회사 ×	스키 ×

1 월요일에는 <u>청소하지 않을 거예요</u>.

2 화요일에는 __________________.

3 수요일에는 __________________.

4 목요일에는 __________________.

5 금요일에는 __________________.

6 토요일에는 __________________.

7 일요일에는 __________________.

라 Read the passage and then use '—지 않다' to answer the questions.

> 지난 주말에 기차로 부산에 갔어요. 부산에서 시내에 가지 않았어요. 바닷가에는 사람이 아주 많았어요. 아주 더웠어요.

1 지난 주말에 제주도에 갔어요?

→ <u>아니요, 지난 주말에 제주도에 가지 않았어요. 부산에 갔어요</u>.

2 부산에 비행기로 갔어요?

→ __________________.

3 부산에서 시내에 갔어요?

→ __________________.

4 바닷가에 사람이 적었어요?

→ __________________.

5 날씨가 따뜻했어요?

→ __________________.

10 V지 마세요

Basic Form	A/V지 말다
Conjugation	V지 마세요 V지 마

And finally there's the negative imperative form. One thing you should notice is that this is rarely conjugated into the '아/어요' form. That's because when you are giving a command to someone, it's best to be polite and use the '(으)세요' ending to people you aren't great friends with. (See Section 7) When you are great friends with them then you just use the lowest form, which simply drops the '세요' at the end.

잊지 마세요.
Don't forget, please.

반바지를 입지 마세요.
Don't wear shorts, please.

Some expressions you can use to children or friends:

울지 마.
Don't cry.

하지 마.
Don't do (that.)

V지 마세요.

늦지 마세요.	Okay, I'll make sure to be on time.
담배를 피우지 마세요.	It's not allowed inside this building.
술을 마시지 마세요.	Why? I don't have to drive tonight.
집에 가지 마세요.	Darn. And I was about to leave for the day.
너무 비싸요. 사지 마세요.	You know we can't afford it.

V지 마!

말하지 마.	It's our little secret.
아직 자지 마.	We're just getting started!
돈을 주지 마.	You've done enough already. Thanks anyway.
버스를 타지 마.	Take the subway instead.
기다리지 마.	Go to sleep. I'll be home soon.

V마[30)

걱정 마.	I'll be fine.

Going Native ~

Our final expression is one you can ONLY use with the best of friends! But you will absolutely crack Koreans up if you pick the right situation to use this one. 웃기다 is to make someone laugh, but when someone says something that is impossible or you totally disagree with, you can say.

웃기지 마! = Don't make me laugh!

---

30) This is the single example of a verb that requires only '마' attached to the end in order to make it into a negative command.

가 Listen carefully and then circle the correct picture.

1 ㄱ)   ㄴ)   ㄷ)

2 ㄱ) 유식 씨가 오늘 밤에 전화하겠습니다.

   ㄴ) 유식 씨가 내일 전화하겠습니다.

   ㄷ) 존이 오늘 밤에 전화하겠습니다.

3 ㄱ)   ㄴ)   ㄷ)

4 Look at the following pictures and use '—지 마세요' to respond to the situation.

1 

2 

울지 마세요 .

________________________ .

3 

4 

________________________ .

________________________ .

5 

________________________ .

 Look at the following pictures and make a sentence using '—지 마세요.'

1 U턴하지 마세요   .

2 _______________________ .

3 _______________________ .

4 _______________________ .

5 _______________________ .

라 **You're talking to a good friend who is your own age. Use '—지 마' to tell her/him not to do something.**

1 (To your friend who is late, but says he's going to ride the bus) 버스 타지 마   .

2 (When your friend has as a lot of things she/he is worried about) _______________ .

3 (Reminding your friend about your birthday) _______________________ .

4 (To your friend who is about to make a phone call late at night)_______________ .

5 (To your friend who is going to a club meeting early) _______________________ .

Section 3
The Basic Markers

11 N이, N가

Usage	받침-ending nouns → N이
	vowel-ending nouns → N가

A crucial concept to understand about Korean is the usage of markers. Korean syntax (word order) is more flexible than English because the subjects are determined by the addition of markers. The most common word order, however, goes subject-object-verb (S-O-V). (English is of course S-V-O.) Korean sentences end with a verb or adjective. Your first set of markers are the subject markers '이' and '가.' They are directly attached after the subject of the sentence. And remember that you have to pronounce the 받침 clearly when it is attached to the 받침 enabling '이.' Another thing to remember is that these markers are sometimes omitted in colloquial speech.

꽃이 예뻐요.[31)]
The flowers are pretty.

---

31) Plurals are not as essential in Korean as they are in English. Sometimes they sound more awkward than natural.

책이 재미있어요.
The book is good.[32]

내일 동생이 와요.
(My) brother comes tomorrow.

시계가 아주 멋있어요.
(That) watch is very cool.

---

32) Literally "The book is fun or entertaining." Perhaps an even better translation would be, "It's a good book."

Extension

N이

형이 나갔어요.	Did he say when he would be back?
음악이 너무 빨라요.	Okay, I'll change the song.
신발이 예뻐요.	Were they expensive?
이게 뭐예요?	It's in the dictionary. Look it up.

N가

친구가 기다려요.	Then you'd better get going.
나무가 많아요.	Is it a park?
날씨가 따뜻해요.	I love this season.
민주가 지금 자요.	Then I'll be quiet.

The subject maker is also used when someone is amongst a group of people and they individuate themselves (or someone else picks them out of the crowd) in some way.

Everyone is getting ready to go on a trip and John wants to do the grocery shopping so he shouts:

제가 쇼핑할게요![33] – 그냥 제가 살게요!

Or when a group is deciding who will call the professor and an older friend volunteers his younger friend Jung-ho's services:

정호 씨가 전화할 거예요.

Or when deciding who will do the cleaning, a volunteer would say:

제가 청소할게요!

Or when the teacher is trying to find a certain student he would ask:

누가 스티븐이에요?[34]

And the answer would be:

제가 스티븐이에요. (NOT 저는 스티븐이에요)

---

33) '(으)ㄹ게요' is a sentence ending expressing that I want to do something if no one else minds.

34) '누구가' is always shortened to '누가.'

 Listen carefully and then circle the correct picture.

1   ㄱ)   ㄴ)   ㄷ)

2   ㄱ)   ㄴ)   ㄷ)

3   ㄱ)   ㄴ)   ㄷ)

 Look at the following pictures and use '**이/가**' to respond to the situation.

1

누가 와요? → ___여자 친구가 와요___ .

2

뭐가 맛있어요? → _______________________ .

3

누가 운전해요? → _______________________ .

4

뭐가 재미있어요? → _______________________ .

5

날씨가 어때요? → _______________________ .

6

이 시계 어때요? → _______________________ .

 Choose whether to use '이' or '가' and then make the sentence.

1 한국 노래, 좋다 → 한국 노래가 좋아요 .

2 이 식당 음식, 맛있다 → _______________________.

3 머리, 아프다 → _______________________.

4 가방, 좋다 → _______________________.

5 동생, 자다 → _______________________.

6 신발, 예쁘다 → _______________________.

 Use either '이' or '가' to answer the question using the supplied subject.

1 누가 와요? → (형) 형이 와요 .

2 누가 공부해요? → (누나) _______________________.

3 뭐가 재미있어요? → (책) _______________________.

4 뭐가 힘들어요? → (일) _______________________.

5 어디가 가까워요? → (일본) _______________________.

6 누가 미국 사람이에요? → (스티븐) _______________________.

12 N을, N를

Usage

받침-ending nouns → N을

vowel-ending nouns → N를

The markers '을' and '를' are attached to the object of the sentence. Generally in English we just use the placing in the sentence - the word order - to signify the object of the sentence. But often we also place articles - a, an, the - before the object and you will see that the objective marker plays a similar role. You will also see in the **Extension** section that sometimes the objective marker plays the same role as some prepositions.

매일 아침을 먹어요.
(I) eat breakfast everyday.

사진을 찍어요.
Take a picture.

영화를 볼 거예요.
(We're) going to watch a movie.

전화번호를 쓰세요.35)
Please write (your) phone number.

---

35) See Section 7 for an explanation of this sentence ending.

N을

한국말을 공부해요.	At this moment, aren't you?
약을 먹었어요.	That's why you look tired.
수업을 잘 들어요.	Don't get distracted.
편의점을 찾고 있어요.	There's one around the corner.

N를

녹차를 마셔요.	It's healthier than coffee.
반바지를 입어요.	It's hot outside.
철수가 미영이를 만났어요.36)	Was it a date? Are they together now?
일요일에 축구를 할 거예요.	Are you in a league?
편지를 받았어요.	You'll have to send a reply now.

Occasionally it will be the equivalent of a preposition in English – to, of, for, in, on, etc.

소풍을 갈 거예요.	Don't do that. It's supposed to rain.
6시간을 자요.	7 or 8 a night is healthier.
음악을 들을 거예요.	Some Mozart perhaps.

Objective Questions37)

어딜 가요?	I'm just gonna grab a coffee.
뭘 해요?	Nothing much.
누굴 기다려요?	The doctor. They're always late.
뭘 먹었어요?	I had some chicken kalbi.

---

36) Koreans often attach '이' on to names ending with a 받침 for people they are friendly with.

37) These are all contractions because people only use the contractions in spoken Korean. The contractions are:
무엇을 → 뭘 / 누구를 → 누굴 / 어디를 → 어딜

가 Listen carefully and then circle the correct one.

1   ㄱ)   ㄴ)   ㄷ)

2   ㄱ)   ㄴ)   ㄷ)

3   ㄱ)   ㄴ)   ㄷ)

4 Look at the following picture and use '을/를' in making your sentence.

1 

<u>잠을 자요</u> .

2 

_________________________ .

3 

_________________________ .

4 

_________________________ .

5 

_________________________ .

6 

_________________________ .

다 Make the following sentences using '을/를.'

1 갈비, 좋아하다   <u>갈비를 좋아해요</u>.

2 감기약, 먹다   ___________________.

3 영화, 보다   ___________________.

4 음악, 듣다   ___________________.

5 친구, 만나다   ___________________.

6 사진, 찍다   ___________________.

라 Use '을/를' to answer the following questions.

1 누구를 기다려요?   → (형) <u>형을 기다려요</u>.

2 누굴 만나요?   → (누나) ___________________.

3 뭘 마실 거예요?   → (맥주) ___________________.

4 뭘 볼 거예요?   → (한국 영화) ___________________.

5 일요일에 뭘 할 거예요?   → (축구) ___________________.

6 뭘 배워요?   → (한국말) ___________________.

Contrastive/Topic Marker

N은, N는

받침-ending nouns → N은
vowel-ending nouns → N는

Now comes the real challenge. This contrastive/topic marker is used to indicate a contrast with something else or bring up a new topic for discussion. Quite often the contrastive/topic markers '은' and '는' are attached to what in English we would generally consider the subject of the sentence, but instead it is the topic. Here are some examples:

저는 미국 사람이에요.[38]
I'm American.

---

38) When introducing yourself, you always use the contrastive/topic marker to talk about yourself. To tell someone your name, it's "저는 스티븐이에요." NOT "제가 스티븐이에요."

이분은 선생님이세요.[39)]
This person is a teacher.

Then there are other times where you are talking about someone's likes, dislikes or interests, and in describing them you are talking about their similarities or differences from others. That is when you're using the 'contrastive' meaning of this marker.

나는 노란색을 좋아해요.
I like yellow.

켈리는 파란색을 좋아해요.
Kelly likes blue.

It is also used to contrast and emphasize the differences or similarities of two things. In these instances the contrastive/topic marker would instead be attached to (what in English would be) the object of the sentence.

김치는 좋아해요.
(I) like kimchi.

그렇지만 닭갈비는 싫어해요.
But (I) don't like chicken kalbi.

---

39) '분' is the honorific form of '사람.' See Section 7, Chapter 27 for more explanation.

Extension

Contrastive 은/는 – Subject of the sentence

지원 씨는 고기를 안 먹어요.[40]	But I love it.
어제 숙제는 아주 어려웠어요.	Tougher than usual, huh?
우리 형은 대학생이에요.[41]	But you're not? Are you still in high school?
이 식당은 아주 맛있어요.	Good. The place yesterday was bland.

Contrastive 은/는 – Objective of the sentence

밥은 먹을 거예요.	What are you going to have?
음악은 안 들려요.	But you can hear me talking, right?
가게는 못 봤어요.	It's just after the pharmacy you passed.
책은 많이 읽었어요.	But you didn't see any movies?

Another challenge presented is that you can also attach the contrastive marker to other markers. Again this is to express a contrast:

처음에는 김치를 못 먹었어요.	But you love it now, don't you?
편의점에선 안 팔아요.[42]	Can we get it at the department store?
대전까지는 KTX로 가요.	So how do you go the rest of the way?
동생에게는 안 보냈어요.	But I sent it to my older sister.
한국말이 나한테는 어려워요.	But it may seem easy to Koreans.

---

40) Notice that these contrastive imply that one person is different in some way from the other people in the group.

41) What's different about the speaker? It means that the speaker doesn't attend university, right? Or it means the person is contrasting his older brother with someone else's sibling.

42) In spoken and even sometimes written Korean '는' will just be abbreviated to a 받침 added to the previous syllable. In this instance '에서는' becomes '에선.' Other examples include '엔', '한텐', and '에겐.' This also goes for '이것은', '그것은', and '저것은', '이건', '그건', and '저건.'

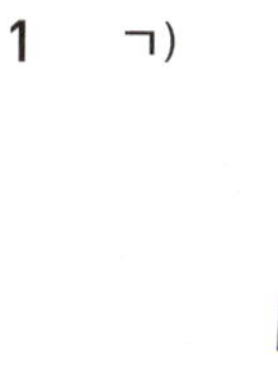 Listen carefully and then circle the correct one.

1   ㄱ)

ㄴ)

ㄷ)

2   ㄱ)

ㄴ)

ㄷ)

3   ㄱ)   ㄴ)   ㄷ)

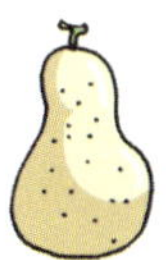

ㄴ Look at the picture, then use the word given and '은/는' to make the sentence.

1 

(저, 이분)   저는 선생님이에요

  이분은 회사원이에요 .

2 

(어머니, 아버지) ___________________

___________________ .

3 

(동생, 형) ___________________

___________________ .

4 

(사과, 딸기) ___________________

___________________ .

5 

(이분, 저분) ___________________

___________________ .

6

(서울, 뉴욕) ___________________

___________________ .

1 한국 음식을 좋아해요? → (냉면) 네, 한국 음식을 좋아해요. 냉면은 안 좋아해요 .

2 음악을 자주 들어요? → (클래식 음악) ________________________________.

3 꽃을 샀어요? → (케이크) ________________________________.

4 가방을 살 거예요? → (구두) ________________________________.

5 이 영화를 볼 거예요? → (저 영화) ________________________________.

6 동생을 만나요? → (형) ________________________________.

라 Use the given word and '은/는' to respond to the question.

1 백화점에서 이 라면을 팔아요? → (편의점) 네, 편의점에서는 안 팔아요 .

2 오늘 숙제가 쉬웠어요? → (어제 숙제) ________________________________.

3 서울이 추워요? → (북경) ________________________________.

4 회사에서 담배를 피워요? → (집) ________________________________.

5 이 책이 재미있어요? → (저 책) ________________________________.

6 이 식당 음식이 맛있어요? → (저 식당) ________________________________.

Section 4
Conjunctive Particles

14 N(이)랑 N, N하고 N, N와/과 N

Conjugation	받침 enabler 이(attached to both nouns) – N(이)랑
	direct attachment – 하고
	opposite of 받침 enabler rule! (the only case) – 와/과

There are a lot of ways to say 'and' in Korean. For combining two nouns (not clauses), for instance, there are three main ways and they're all used just a little bit differently, and to drive you even crazier, they're all conjugated differently.

The most casual way to say 'and' is 'N(이)랑.' It is usually used with friends. When conjugating you only add the '이' when the noun you're attaching it to has a 받침 the 받침 enabler '이.' The other key is that often it is attached to both of the nouns that you are referring to.

사진이랑 비디오를 찍었어요.
(They) took pictures and video.

혜숙이랑 승주가 대학교에서 가르쳐요.
Hye-sook and Seung-joo teach at university.

Here's the easiest and most common one. 'N하고' is just attached to the noun regardless of whether there is a 받침 or not. It's also the most common and probably the safest way to go in all situations.

밥하고 김치 먹어요.
(I) eat kimchi and rice.

운동화하고 구두를 살 거예요.
(I'm) going to buy gym shoes and dress shoes.

Our final way of saying 'and' is more formal and is written much more often than it is spoken. Sadly, contrary to all that you've learned up to now, 'N와/과' are attached in the opposite format of the 받침 enabler rule that I've touted so much. When the noun it is attached to has a 받침, then you attach '과.' When the noun it is attached to ends in a vowel, then you add '와.' Go figure!

회사와 학교가 가까워요.
The school and the company
are near (each other).

지하철과 버스를 탔어요.
(I) rode the subway and the bus.

And all of these can be used the same way we would use 'with' in English - just don't add a second noun.

친구랑 학교에 갔어요.
(I) went to school with
(my) friend.

엄마하고 쇼핑 갈 거예요.
(I'm) going to go shopping
with (my) mom.

대통령과 인터뷰하고
있어요.
(They're) interviewing
the president.

N(이)랑

백화점이랑 슈퍼마켓이 있어요.	That's a convenient area.
이름이랑 나이를 쓰세요.	On this form.
가격이랑 디자인이 정말 괜찮아요.	It's a very reasonable purchase.
동생이랑 동생의 남자친구가 집에 왔어요.	Are they dating that seriously?

N하고

전화하고 침대를 샀어요.	You have to buy a lot of stuff when you move, don't you?
간호사하고 의사가 아주 좋아요.	That's why I like that hospital.
상추하고 삼겹살을 주세요.[43]	I'm having a party.
아침하고 저녁에 약을 드세요.	Before or after meals?

N와/과

한국과 일본은 가까워요.	Their languages are similar too.
은행은 서점과 우체국 사이에 있어요.	You can't miss it. The ATMs are in front.
러시아와 중국을 여행할 거예요.	By train by any chance?
봄과 가을에 날씨가 좋아요.	Summer and winter, however, aren't so nice.

'With' meaning

여자 친구하고 싸웠어요.	Why? What did she do?
그 사람하고 가세요.	He knows the way.
택시 기사랑 이야기 많이 했어요.	That must have shortened the ride.
한국 친구랑 사귀었어요.	Great! Make sure to speak Korean together.

---

43) '삼겹살' is often called 'Korean bacon' but it's not cured at all, so it's not really bacon. It's the same cut of meat, however, and wrapped up in lettuce, it's one of the favorite foods for parties.

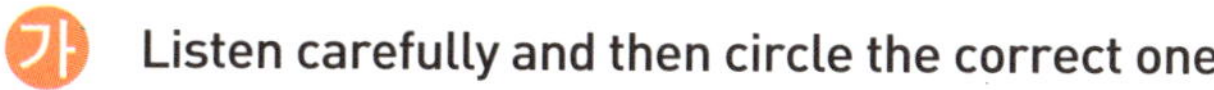 Listen carefully and then circle the correct one.

1 ㄱ)  ㄴ)  ㄷ) 

2 ㄱ) 한국어와 일본어를 해요.

ㄴ) 일본어와 중국어를 해요.

ㄷ) 독일어와 일본어를 해요.

3 ㄱ)  ㄴ)  ㄷ) 

나 Look at the following picture and use '—(이)랑', '하고' or '와/과' to make a sentence.

1

사과랑 딸기를 사요. / 사과하고 딸기를
사요. / 사과와 딸기를 사요 .

2

____

_______________________ .

3

____

_______________________ .

4

____

_______________________ .

5

____

_______________________ .

6

____

_______________________ .

 Use the given words and '하고' to make a sentence.

1 시장에서 샀어요.

(사과/배) _시장에서 사과하고 배를 샀어요_.

2 백화점에서 살 거예요.

(가방/시계) ________________________.

3 다음 주에 여행할 거예요.

(제주도/부산) ________________________.

4 회사에 가요.

(지하철/버스) ________________________.

5 여기에 쓰세요.

(이름/주소) ________________________.

6 다음 주말에 만나요.

(승주/마이클) ________________________.

라 **Respond to the following questions using '—(이)랑', '하고' or '와/과.'**

1 일본에 어떻게 갔어요?　　　　　　　→ (기차/배) _기차하고 배로 갔어요_.

2 백화점에서 뭘 샀어요?　　　　　　　→ (넥타이/지갑) ________________.

3 이번 여름에 어디를 여행할 거예요? → (베트남/캄보디아) ________________.

4 누가 집에 왔어요?　　　　　　　　　→ (동생/동생 여자 친구) ____________.

5 누구하고 영화를 볼 거예요?　　　　→ (동생) ________________________.

6 누구랑 싸웠어요?　　　　　　　　　→ (앞집 아줌마) ________________.

N or N (N or something)

N(이)나

Conjugation

받침-ending nouns → N이나

vowel-ending nouns → N나

Then there are those occasions when you have to choose between two things.

생선이나 소고기가 있어요.
(We) have fish or beef.

우유나 설탕 필요해요?
Would (you) like milk or sugar?

That may seem easy, but this ending also has some other usages. Sometimes it's not two choices, but there are a few choices that you could make, and then it's meaning is more like 'or something like that.' Or something along those lines:

우리 차나 한잔해요.[44)]
Let's have tea or something?

주말에 친구나 만날 거예요.
On the weekend (I) will meet a friend or something.

---

44) 한잔하다 - to have a drink - As with English this frequently means to drink alcohol, but if you mention coffee or tea in front of it you are showing that you want to drink something besides alcohol.

N이나 - 받침 ending

노트북이나 PC를 살까요?[45]	Desktops or towers are cheaper.
화요일이나 수요일에 할 거예요.	The sooner the better.
술이나 담배 많이 하면 안 좋아요.	Moderation is the key.
중국이나 싱가포르를 여행할 거예요.	Looking to practice your Mandarin?
노란색이나 빨간색이 있어요.	Don't you have blue?

N나 - vowel ending

서강대나 서울대에서 한국어를 공부할 거예요.	They're both good choices.
주말에는 비디오나 디비디를 봐요.	Don't you ever go out?
저녁에 숙제나 운동을 해요.	Really? I just watch TV.
이메일이나 팩스로 보내세요.	I'll do it first thing when I get to the office.

N(이)나 - ~or something

주말에 등산이나 갈 거예요.	Which mountain are you headed to?
밥이나 먹을까요?	I'm pretty full. Raincheck?
방학에 영어 공부나 할 거예요.	Really? I'm giving my brain a rest.
영화나 볼까요?	Okay. But just as friends. Don't expect a goodnight kiss.

Going Native ~

Now for a key phrase to learn. Guess what this one could mean:

당신 일이나 하세요. = **Mind your own business.**

Be careful to use it sparingly, if at all! You could really offend someone with this one.

---

45) This sentence ending is used so commonly with this grammar that we had to give these examples. It means 'Shall we V?' or 'Should we V?'

가 **Listen and choose the thing <u>NOT</u> discussed.**

1   ㄱ)   ㄴ)   ㄷ)

2   ㄱ)   ㄴ)   ㄷ)

3   ㄱ)   ㄴ)   ㄷ)

녹차   커피   홍차

4 Answer the following questions according to the pictures.

1

뭘 마셔요?

→ ____콜라나 오렌지 주스를 마셔요____ .

2

주말에 뭘 해요?

→ ________________________ .

3

이번 겨울에 어디를 여행해요?

→ ________________________ .

4

언제 파티를 해요?

→ ________________________ .

5
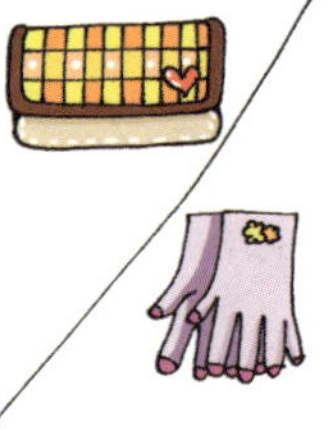

친구 생일에 무슨 선물을 줘요?

→ ________________________ .

6

무슨 운동을 해요?

→ ________________________ .

다 Use 'N(이)나' with the given words to complete the sentences.

1 (불고기/라면) 점심으로 __불고기나 라면을__ 먹어요.

2 (맥주/와인) 오늘은 ________________ 마셔요.

3 (운동/서울 구경) 주말에 친구하고 ________________ 할 거예요.

4 (이번 주말/다음 주말) 제 생일 파티는 ________________ 할 거예요.

5 (구두/옷) 동생 생일에 ________________을 줄 거예요.

6 (영어 공부/일본어 공부) 방학에 ________________ 할 거예요.

라 Use 'N(이)나' and the given words to answer the questions.

1 부모님께 어떻게 연락해요?

   → (전화/이메일) __전화나 이메일로 연락해요__________.

2 무슨 영화 볼 거예요?

   → (한국 영화/일본 영화) ________________.

3 옷은 어디에서 사요?

   → (시장/백화점) ________________.

4 시간이 있으면 뭐 해요?

   → (영화/공연) ________________.

5 주말에 뭐 할 거예요?

   → (비디오) ________________.

6 이번 여름에 뭐 할 거예요?

   → (여행) ________________.

N too/also, N either, even

N도

It doesn't get much easier than this one. You simply attach '도' directly on to the noun to say 'too.'

My Korean students, when learning English, would often say something like, "I don't like it too." I couldn't figure out why they kept doing this until I learned enough Korean to realize that it is because they 'too' and 'either/neither' are the same attachment in Korean! Now I get it just fine.

One of the most common phrases you will ever hear in Korea:

나도요.[46)]
Me too. (Me either.)

---

46) You'll hear it pronounced "나두요." a lot. They're being cute when they do that. The correct pronunciation is "나도요." You can drop the '요' when you're with close friends too. And when you're with a much senior person, you should say, "저도요."

내 동생도 고등학생이에요.
My younger sibling is a high school student too.

은주 씨도 간호사예요.
Eunjoo is a nurse too.

And 'N도' is often also used the way that we use 'even' in English.

그 슈퍼마켓에서 샌드위치도 팔아요.
That supermarket even sells sandwiches.

Extension

N도 – too

존 씨의 여자 친구도 왔어요.	Great, I've wanted to meet her.
아침하고 저녁에도 운동해요.	That's how you stay in such great shape.
넥타이도 사세요.	This suit was expensive! Just throw one in.
노래하고 춤도 출 거예요.	I'm looking forward to your performance.
명동에도 갈 거예요.[47]	That's going to take a lot of time.

N도 – either

민주도 안 해요.	Then who will help out?
나도 숙제하지 않았어요.	Did the class all go out together last night?
우리 언니도 돈이 없어요.	Then I'll loan you the money for today.
학교에도 그 책이 없어요.	You'll have to go to The National Library.

N도 – even

회사에도 안 가요.	You must have really been sick.
나는 돈이 10원도 없어요.	In that case, I'll buy lunch.
한 번도 안 갔어요.	Oh, you've gotta try that place.
하나도 몰라요.[48]	I'll teach you.

Going Native ~

Here's a little proverb/saying for you:

원숭이도 나무에서 떨어진다.[49] = Everyone can make a mistake sometimes.

---

47) Notice that you can attach it after the postpositions as well.

48) A bit of an idiomatic expression. Can you figure out what it means?

49) '원숭이' means monkey. '떨어진다' means to fall from. Get it? 'Even monkeys fall from trees.'

가 Listen carefully and then choose the correct answer.

1 ㄱ) 이 식당은 값이 비싸요.

   ㄴ) 이 식당은 음식이 맛있어요.

   ㄷ) 이 식당은 집에서 멀어요.

2 ㄱ) 메리는 한국에 안 갔어요.

   ㄴ) 메리는 일본에 안 갔어요.

   ㄷ) 메리는 중국에 안 갔어요.

3 ㄱ) 영숙이가 안 왔어요.

   ㄴ) 메리가 안 왔어요.

   ㄷ) 존이 안 왔어요.

나 Look at the following pictures and use '—도' to answer the question.

1 

2 

어제는 집에서 쉬었어요. 유식 씨는요?[50]

→ ___저도 쉬었어요___________________________.

제 동생은 키가 작아요. 유식 씨 동생은요?

→ _______________________________________.

50) You can just add the contrastive marker in this way to ask 'How about N?' or 'What about N?'

3

저는 노래를 좋아해요. 유식 씨는요?

→ ________________________________ .

4

저는 숙제를 안 했어요. 유식 씨는요?

→ ________________________________ .

5

저는 자전거를 못 타요. 유식 씨는요?

→ ________________________________ .

6

우리 형은 주말에 등산해요. 유식 씨 형은요?

→ ________________________________ .

다 Put the correct marker(도, 은, or 는) in the parenthesis.

1 이것은 영숙 씨 시계예요.

저것(은) 영숙 씨 시계가 아니에요.

이것(도) 영숙 씨 시계가 아니에요.

2 지혜 씨는 한국 사람이에요.

철수 씨(　　) 한국 사람이에요.

윌슨 씨(　　) 영국 사람이에요.

3 유식 씨는 매운 음식을 잘 먹어요.

지혜 씨(　　) 매운 음식을 잘 못 먹어요.

윌슨 씨(　　) 매운 음식을 잘 못 먹어요.

4 저는 한국어를 공부해요.

윌슨 씨(　　) 한국어를 공부해요.

존 씨(　　) 한국어를 공부해요.

라 Complete the sentence.

1 윌슨 씨는 대학교에서 한국어를 배워요.

존슨 씨도 ___대학교에서 한국어를 배워요___.

저는 ___대학교에서 한국어를 안 배워요___.

2 윌슨 씨는 영화를 좋아해요.

유식 씨도 ______________________.

저는 ______________________.

3 유식 씨는 도서관에 가지 않아요.

저도 ______________________.

존 씨도 ______________________.

4 어제는 추웠어요.

오늘도 ______________________.

내일은 ______________________.

17 N의 N

| Usage | Direct attachment to noun → N의 |

This one is not so tough for the most part. To make the possessive form of a noun all you have to do is add a '의' to the end of the noun just like we add a 's after a noun. Of course there is a glitch. It is almost never pronounced [의] as it would be in '의자.' Except on the news or in other very official situations it is always pronounced [에].

오늘의 스프는 양파 스프예요.
Today's soup is onion soup.

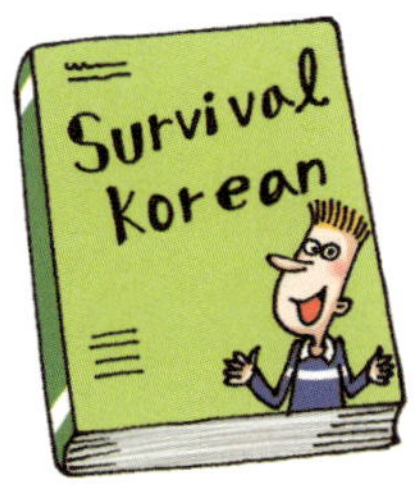

이것이 스티븐의 책이에요.
This is Stephen's book.

One thing you will soon realize is that the possessive form is not nearly as necessary as it is in English. More often than not it's meaning is implied - meaning '의' is more often than not omitted.

이것은 누구(의) 책이에요?
Whose book is this?

이건 지혜 씨(의) 가방이에요.[51]
This is Ji-hye's bag.

Now there are some pronouns that get substituted for this as well:

Honorific form:
I = 저 → 저의 → 제 = my   저의 책이에요. = 제 책이에요.

With friends:
I = 나 → 나의 → 내 = my   나의 방이에요. = 내 방이에요.

To children or your closest friends:
You = 너 → 너의 → 네 = your   너의 옷이니? = 네 옷이니?[52]

---

51) Here the original is '이것은' but as often happens Koreans save having to pronounce an extra syllable by making it '이건.'

52) Since the sound of the vowels '에' and '애' are almost the same, Koreans often differentiate from '내' (my) and '네' (your) by pronouncing '네' as [니]. This inadvertently got them into trouble when speaking to black people because, when combined with the subject marker '네가' it can be misinterpreted by someone who doesn't know Korean as a racial slur!

N의 – N's

컴퓨터의 문제가 뭐예요?	I have no idea. These things hate me.
재운이의 여자 친구가	Oh, an international relationship.
일본 사람이에요.	
대구의 사과가 제일 맛있어요.[53]	Yes, they're famous.
한국의 음식이 맛있어요.	And healthy for the most part too.

Omitted '의'

그 사람은 누구 오빠예요?[54]	I'm not sure.
선영 씨 오빠예요.	Oh, now I see the resemblance.
이게 유식이 오토바이예요.	When did he buy that? Isn't it dangerous?
이 방은 동생 방이에요.	Where is yours? Is it this next one?

Possessive Pronouns

제 이름은 제임스예요.	Nice to meet you.
제 형이 회사원이에요.	Is he married yet?
내 거예요.[55]	Don't mess with it.
내 일이 아직 안 끝났어요.	Wait a few more minutes and I'll join you.

Going Native ~

when you'd like to politely give your opinion you can start the sentence like so:

제 생각에는 어려울 거예요.[56] = In my opinion, it'll be difficult.

내 생각에는 맛이 없어요. = In my opinion, it's not very good.

---

53) The city of Taegu is famous for just this sort of thing.

54) It is especially uncommon for people to add '의' to '누구.' It is nearly always omitted.

55) The noun '것' is shortened to '거' after a possessive.

56) '생각' literally means thought or idea - but in this case you're giving your opinion.

가 Listen carefully and then circle the correct one.

1 ㄱ) 켈리 차   ㄴ) 켈리 어머니 차   ㄷ) 켈리 동생 차

2 ㄱ) 영숙 씨 친구   ㄴ) 남편 친구   ㄷ) 영숙 씨 남편

3 ㄱ) 내 거   ㄴ) 유식 씨 거   ㄷ) 유식 씨 친구 거

나 Who do the following belong to? Answer the question according to the picture.

1 

2 

유식 씨의 책이에요   .   ________________________.

3

__________________________.

4

__________________________.

5

__________________________.

다 Use the word provided to answer the question.

1 이건 누구 책이에요? → (저) <u>저의/제 책이에요</u>.

2 저건 누구 지갑이에요? → (나) ____________________.

3 여긴 누구 집이에요? → (존) ____________________.

4 이분은 누구 부인이에요? → (재운) ____________________.

5 이분은 누구 어머니예요? → (메리) ____________________.

라 Answer the following in two different ways as shown in the example.

1 이건 누구 컴퓨터예요?

→ (메리) <u>이건 메리 컴퓨터예요. / 이건 메리 거예요</u>.

2 이건 누구 안경이에요?

→ (유식) ____________________.

3 저건 누구 휴대전화예요?

→ (존) ____________________.

4 저건 누구 차예요?

→ (영숙) ____________________.

5 그건 누구 잡지예요?

→ (윌슨) ____________________.

Section 5
Postpositions

18 P에게, P한테, P께

We translated this one to the preposition 'to' but you should be careful to pay attention to one crucial factor - it is only used for 'to' a person. You never use this postposition to talk about going 'to' a place or other situations that we might use the English preposition for.

You'll also notice that we have three versions of the same thing. The first two 'P에게' and 'P한테' are interchangeable, but '한테' is a little more common in colloquial Korean. 'P께' on the other hand, is the honorific ending with the same meaning - so as with all honorifics it is used for people who are in a higher status than you are due to age, rank, etc.

They're all relatively easy to use:

언니한테 말했어요.
(I) told (my) older sister.

편지를 남자 친구에게 보냈어요.
(I) sent a letter to (my) boyfriend.

지혜 씨한테 전화했어요?
Did (you) call Ji-hye?

어머니께 드리세요.[57]
Give (it) to your mother.

부모님께 선물을 드렸어요.
(I) gave a present to (my) parents.

---

57) See Section 7 for more explanation of honorifics.

Extension

Speaking to someone

친구에게 물어보세요.	She might know.
나한테 거짓말을 하지 마세요.	I'll never trust you again if you do.
친구에게 말을 할까요?	Of course. His wife is cheating on him.
선생님께 말씀을 드려요.58)	I'll be back at school tomorrow.

This postposition is also used a lot when talking about ownership using 있다 or 없다 in substitution of the contrastive/topic marker (See Section 3). 한테 is used more often in this situation.

그 사진이 누구한테 있어요?	I'd really love a copy.
지금 저에게 없어요.	I'll get it for you later.
열쇠가 언니한테 있어요.	I can't get into the house.
제 휴대전화가 선생님께 있어요.	It rang in class and she took it.

This phrase is also used in a lot of sentences where we would not say the 'to' in English.

저한테 기회를 주세요.	You won't regret it.
동생한테 정말 미안해요.	I broke his toy.
외국 사람에게 한국어를 가르쳐요.	That doesn't pay very well, does it?
우리 딸에게 그 일을 시켰어요.59)	She'll do a great job.

It doesn't have to be a specific person all the time, it could be a general group of people.

그 가게는 손님에게 친절해요.	Their service is the best.
그 음식이 여자에게 안 좋아요.	Is it okay for men to eat it?
한국말이 외국인에게 어려워요.	It sure is, isn't it?
우리 가족한테 보내요.	They'll love it.

Going Native ~

In Korean you don't ask someone to say hello for you, you ask them to send your regards.

안부 전해 주세요. = Tell him / her I said "Hi."

---

58) See Section 7 for more explanation of honorifics.

59) 시키다 - to make someone do something.

가 Listen carefully and then circle the correct picture.

1 ㄱ)   ㄴ)   ㄷ)

2 ㄱ)   ㄴ)   ㄷ)

3 ㄱ)   ㄴ)   ㄷ)

 What is 유식 doing? Look at the picture and use '에게/한테/께' to make a sentence.

1 

유식 씨가 정희한테 / 정희에게 전화해요 .

2 

_______________________ .

3 

_______________________ .

4 

_______________________ .

5 

_______________________ .

다 Use the given word and '한테/께' to make a sentence.

1 어제 전화했어요.　　　　　→ (언니) ___어제 언니한테 전화했어요___.

2 편지를 썼습니다.　　　　　→ (남자 친구) _______________________.

3 선물을 보냈습니다.　　　　→ (부모님) _______________________.

4 질문했어요.　　　　　　　→ (선생님) _______________________.

5 한국말이 어려워요.　　　　→ (외국 사람) _______________________.

라 Make the appropriate question for the given answer using '에게/한테.'

1 가: ___누구한테 이 선물을 줄 거예요___?
　　나: 친구한테 이 선물을 줄 거예요.

2 가: _______________________?
　　나: 부모님께 전화할 거예요.

3 가: _______________________?
　　나: 동생한테 옷을 줘요.

4 가: _______________________?
　　나: 그 사진은 친구한테 있어요.

5 가: _______________________?
　　나: 존한테 한국말을 가르쳐요.

19 N에, N에서

Usage

Direct connection

N에 is for the location of things

N에서 is for the location of the occurrence of actions

N에 can also be the equivalent of a variety of propositions

Remembering that cautionary point above is the key to differentiating between these postpositions well. First of all, '에' is used for the location of things, like 'at home' or 'in the park' (see Section 5). Next it is used for times, like 'at five o'clock' and so on. It is also used when talking about what something is good or bad 'for.'

'에서' has two main usages. First of all, whereas '에' talks about the location of a thing, '에서' gives the location for an action's occurrence. Secondly, when you are talking about the location where something originated from, you always use '에서.' Hence, when you use the verb '가다' you always use 'N에 가다' but when you are coming from some place, you always use 'N에서 오다.'

그 레스토랑이 강남에 있어요.
That restaurant is in Kangnam.

아빠가 회사에 가셨어요.
Dad went to the office.

브로콜리가 건강에 좋아요.
Broccoli is good for (your) health.

헬스장에서 운동했어요.
(I) exercised at the health club.

네팔에서 왔어요.
(I) am from Nepal.

N에 – For Location & Destination

명동에 사람들이 많아요.	They're packed like sardines.
명숙이가 편의점에 갔어요.	We ran out of sugar.
그 호텔이 용산구에 있어요.	I'll tell the taxi driver.

N에 – For Time

아침 일곱 시에 학교에 가요.	That's early!
영화가 여섯 시에 시작할 거예요.	Then we'd better get going.
여름에 비가 많이 와요.	Don't lose your umbrella.

N에 – Objective of phrase

담배가 건강에 나빠요.	But I know it's tough to quit.
당근이 눈에 좋아요.	They say rabbits have perfect vision.
삼계탕이 몸에 좋아요.[60]	Chicken soup is popular everywhere for health.

N에서 – Location of an action's occurrence

신촌에서 만나요.	Okay. What time?
회사에서 일해요.	Full time or part time?
집에서 쉬었어요.	All weekend? You should get out more.

N에서 – Origins

어디에서 왔어요?	I can tell from your accent you're not from these parts.
베트남에서 왔어요.	Welcome to Korea.
집에서 학교까지 30분 걸려요.	That's a long walk.

Going Native ~

'첫' means first. '눈' is eyes. '반하다' is 'to fall in love.'

첫눈에 반했어요. = (I) fell in love at first sight.

---

60) '몸'(body) is often used for talking about your body's health in general.

 ## Skills Building

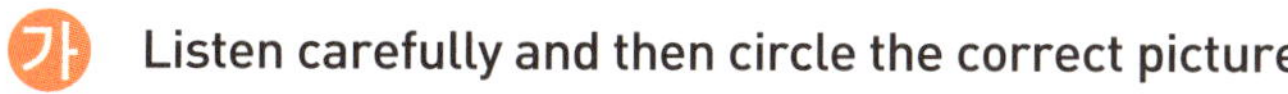 **가** Listen carefully and then circle the correct picture.

1   ㄱ)

ㄴ)

ㄷ)

2   ㄱ)

ㄴ)

ㄷ)

3   ㄱ)

ㄴ)

ㄷ)

나 Where is 지혜 going? Look at the picture and use 'N에' to make a sentence.

1 

지혜 씨가 도서관에 가요   .

2 

                                        .

3 

                                        .

4 

                                        .

다 What is 지혜 doing? Look at the picture and use 'N에서.'

1 

지혜 씨가 도서관에서 책을 읽어요   .

2 

                                        .

3 

                                        .

4 

                                        .

라 **Make a sentence with the given word.**

1 누나가 있어요. (집) _누나가 집에 있어요_ .
2 언니가 갔어요. (회사) ______________________ .
3 한국 노래를 불렀어요. (노래방) ______________________ .
4 주말에 쉬었어요. (집) ______________________ .
5 제 친구가 왔어요. (미국) ______________________ .
6 영화가 시작해요. (5시) ______________________ .

마 **Answer the following question using the given word.**

1 어디에서 일해요? → (자동차 회사) _자동차 회사에서 일해요_ .
2 주말에 어디에 갔어요? → (명동) ______________________ .
3 어디에서 왔어요? → (독일) ______________________ .
4 그 호텔은 어디에 있어요? → (광화문) ______________________ .
5 친구가 언제 한국에 와요? → (다음 주 화요일) ______________________ .
6 어디에서 운동해요? → (헬스장) ______________________ .

바 **Look at the following picture and use '앞에, 옆에, 밑에, 위에, 뒤에, 사이에' to answer the question.**

1 (위에) _책상 위에 열쇠가 있어요_ . 2 (앞에) ______________________ .
3 (옆에) ______________________ . 4 (밑에) ______________________ .
5 (사이에) ______________________ . 6 (뒤에) ______________________ .

I'll take N, by N, to N

20 N(으)로

Conjugation	받침-ending nouns – N(으)로
	vowel-ending nouns – N로

'으로' indicates that a choice has been made for a means of doing something. In situations where there are a few options and one of those options is chosen, then this is your postposition. When the noun ends in a 받침, then you place the '으' in between the noun and '로.' When it ends in a vowel, then you can simply tack on '로.'

There are a few ways to make some things:

손으로 만들어요.
(They) make (it) by hand.

For starters, you often have a choice of transportation:

지하철로 갔어요.[61]
(I) went by subway.

---

61) There is one exception to this rule. Due to naturally occurring pronunciation difficulties, when the word ends in a '르' 받침 then you do not add the '으' in the middle. Some examples include '지하철로', '한국말로.'

Or ways to say things:

You could also be shopping and the store may have a large selection to choose from. Pick one:

But the most common thing you have to do is pick a direction or a place you are going to:

Extension

For Means of Transportation

버스로 왔어요.	Was there much traffic?
자동차로 회사에 다녀요.	How long is the commute?
기차로 갈 거예요.	That's a great way to see the scenery on the way.
자전거로 학교에 다녀요.	Good for your health and the environment.

For Means of Doing Things

영어로 말해요.	It'll be easier for me.
디카로 사진 찍었어요.[62]	Then I'll send you a pic by email.
인터넷으로 찾으세요.	I want to settle this bet.
이메일로 파일을 보내요.	I need your resume ASAP.

Choosing among Many

검은색으로 할게요.	It's better looking than the white.
비싼 것으로 사세요.[63]	The quality is usually better.
그걸로 주세요.[64]	I like that one.
맥주로 주세요.	Soju is too strong for me.

Places you're headed

오른쪽으로 가세요.	At this corner?
왼쪽으로 가세요.	At the next corner?
학교로 갈 거예요.	What time are you headed out?
러시아로 가요.	For vacation?

Going Native ~

There are a few key expressions that use this postposition that you should memorize too.

앞으로 = from now on   처음으로 = for the first time

다음으로 = for the next one, next of all

---

62) 디카 = 디지털 카메라

63) You'll find a more detailed explanation of how to put an adjective before a noun in the next section.

64) '그것으로' is the original format, but that is commonly contracted into the much easier to pronounce '그걸로.'

 **Skills Building**

 Listen carefully and then circle the correct picture.

1   ㄱ)   ㄴ)   ㄷ)

2   ㄱ)   ㄴ)   ㄷ)

3   ㄱ)   ㄴ)   ㄷ)

4 Look at the picture and use 'N(으)로' to make a sentence.

1

학교에 자전거로 가요 .

2

________________________ .

3

________________________ .

4

________________________ .

5

________________________ .

다 **Make a sentence using 'N(으)로' and the given word.**

1 한국 사람은 밥을 먹어요.　(수저)　한국 사람은 수저로 밥을 먹어요 .

2 친구하고 말해요.　(일본어) .

3 이게 뭐예요?　(한국말) .

4 그 사람을 만났어요.　(처음) .

5 회사에 다녀요.　(지하철) .

라 **Answer the following question using 'N(으)로' and the given word.**

1 한국에 어떻게 왔어요?
→ (비행기)　비행기로 왔어요 .

2 부산에 어떻게 갔어요?
→ (기차) .

3 어느 것으로 하겠어요? 노란색? 빨간색?
→ (빨간색) .

4 어디로 가요?
→ (집) .

5 마이클 씨하고 어떻게 말해요?
→ (한국어) .

Section 6
Adnominal Endings

Adjective + Noun

A(으)ㄴ N

Conjugation	받침-ending adjectives – A은 N
	vowel-ending adjectives – Aㄴ N
	Adjectives-ending in 있다/없다 – 있는 N/ 없는 N

Normally verbs and adjectives come at the end of the sentence in Korean, right? Good. I'm glad you've got that down. But sometimes you may want to put an adjective right before a noun - like 'pretty woman.' In this case you need to add a little something directly to the root of the adjective - ㄴ. If the adjective root ends in a 받침, then you need to enable the pronunciation of that 받침 by adding '은.'

예쁘 + ㄴ = 예쁜

→ 예쁜 여자예요.
(She is) a pretty woman.

작 + 은 = 작은

→ 작은 가게가 많아요.
(There are) a lot of small stores.

행복하 + ㄴ = 행복한
→ 행복한 아기예요.
(That) is a happy baby.

복잡하 + ㄴ = 복잡한
→ 남대문 시장은 복잡한 곳이에요.
Namdaemun Market is a crowded place.

'있다' and '없다' can also be made into adjectives, but they have a special format. You have to add '는' onto the end of them. There are also a few nouns that can exist or not exist inherently in something - they would be simple adjective if translated into English. They are '재미'(fun), '멋'(style), and '맛'(taste).

재미없 + 는 = 재미없는
→ 재미없는 영화였어요.
That movie was terrible.
(Literally, "No fun.")

Extension

A ㄴ N

그 사람은 아주 바쁜 사람이에요.	It's tough to get an appointment with him.
조용한 생활이 좋아요.	Not a big party-goer I assume.
큰 집에서 살아요.	Isn't it a little big for one person?

A은 N

인기 많은 프로그램이에요.	Every Thursday people rush home to see it.
짧은 치마 많이 입어요.	Aren't they cold when they wear those?
괜찮은 사람이에요.	Try dating him.

있는/없는 N

고기 없는 비빔밥 주세요.	I'm a vegetarian.
멋있는 옷이에요.	You're always so well dressed.
맛있는 집이에요.	The food is always great at this restaurant.

Irregular Adjectives

Irregular ㅂ (drop the ㅂ and add 우)

어려운 질문이에요.	There's no exact answer.
한국에 매운 음식이 많아요.	Make sure you've got plenty of water.

Irregular ㄹ omission (before ㄴ, omit ㄹ)

힘든 일이에요.	It's very draining.
단 음식을 좋아해요.	Watch out for cavities!

어떤 N[65]

어떤 사람이 좋아요?	I've got a friend to set you up with.
어떤 프로를 볼 거예요?	I prefer news or comedy.
어떤 곳이에요?	I still don't quite understand why it's so popular.

Going Native ~

Here's an old proverb that has an English equivalent that is phrased very differently:

싼 게 비지떡이다.[66] = You get what you pay for.

---

65) '어떻다' originally means 'what kind of' or 'how' but it is an irregular 'ㅎ' verb. When you tack on the 'ㄴ' instead of the 'ㅎ' it turns into a single word asking, 'What kind of N.'

66) '비지떡' is a cheap artificial rice cake made not from rice but bean curd dregs.

 Listen carefully and then circle the correct picture.

1   ㄱ)      ㄴ)      ㄷ)   

2   ㄱ)      ㄴ)      ㄷ)   

3   ㄱ)      ㄴ)      ㄷ)   

나 Look at the following pictures and use 'A(으)ㄴ N' to answer the question.

1

어떤 남자가 좋아요?

→ ___키가 큰 남자가 좋아요___ .

2

어떤 남자가 좋아요?

→ _________________________ .

3

어떤 날씨가 좋아요?

→ _________________________ .

4

어떤 날씨가 좋아요?

→ _________________________ .

5

어떤 음식이 좋아요?

→ _________________________ .

6

어떤 음식이 좋아요?

→ _________________________ .

다 Use 'A(으)ㄴ N' and the given word to answer the following questions.

1 그 영화가 어땠어요?　　　　　→ (재미있다)　 재미있는 영화였어요 　　.

2 존 씨가 키가 커요?　　　　　→ (키가 크다) 네, ＿＿＿＿＿＿＿＿＿.

3 남대문 시장이 복잡해요!　　　→ (복잡하다) 네, ＿＿＿＿＿＿＿＿＿.

4 어떤 음식을 좋아해요?　　　　→ (달다) ＿＿＿＿＿＿＿＿＿＿＿.

5 설악산이 어때요?　　　　　　→ (아름답다) ＿＿＿＿＿＿＿＿＿＿.

라 Use 'A(으)ㄴ N' to answer the following questions.

1 유식 씨가 친절해요?　　　　→ 네, 아주 ＿ 친절한 ＿ 사람이에요.

2 그 김치가 매워요?　　　　　→ 네, 아주 ＿＿＿＿＿ 김치예요.

3 그 케이크가 맛있어요?　　　→ 네, ＿＿＿＿＿＿ 케이크예요.

4 이 시계가 비싸요?　　　　　→ 네, 정말 ＿＿＿＿＿ 시계예요.

5 질문이 어려워요?　　　　　→ 네, ＿＿＿＿＿＿ 질문이에요.

The N(one) that Ved

V(으)ㄴ N

Conjugation

받침-ending verbs → V은
vowel-ending verbs → Vㄴ

Now in the previous section, adjectives are always conjugated the same way when they modify nouns. For verbs, on the other hand, it gets harder, but that's because they convey more meaning - they tell when the action took place. That constantly repeating rule of conjugation comes up again - in the case of a root ending in a 받침, add the 받침 enabler vowel. Past tense actions are conjugated in the same way as adjectives. So when you want to talk about 'the performance that one saw,' you would say:

현주가 본 공연이 재미없었어요.
The performance that Hyun-joo saw
was not good.

제가 말한 친구예요.
This is the friend I told (you) about.

지난주에 먹은 음식이
맛이 없었어요.
The food (we) ate last week was
terrible.

어제 들은 라디오 프로가
웃겼어요.[67]
The radio program (I) listened to
yesterday was funny.

---

67) '듣다' is an irregular 'ㄷ' 받침 verb. See Section 8.

Extension

V ㄴ

남자 친구에게 쓴 이메일이 길었어요.	Writing shorter, frequent emails is better.
오늘 탄 비행기가 복잡했어요.	I hope you got an aisle seat.
백화점에서 산 신발이 마음에 안 들어요.	Too bad. I hope they weren't expensive.

V 은

아침에 먹은 계란이 맛이 있었어요.	That's always tasty in the morning.
어제 읽은 책이 좋았어요.	Glad you enjoyed it.
민호가 신은 운동화가 멋있어요.	He'll be popular at the gym.[68]
치마를 입은 여자가 섹시해요.[69]	Many men think so.

Irregular Verbs

ㄹ omission (just drop ㄹ and add ㄴ)

(만들다) 내가 만든 아이스크림이에요.[70]	That's lots of work when you can just buy it.
(팔다) 친구에게 판 차가 좋았어요.	She must appreciate the deal you gave her.

ㄷ 받침

(걷다) 같이 걸은 바닷가가 아름다웠어요.	That was a scenic area, wasn't it?
(듣다) 지금 들은 노래가 누구 노래예요?	I'm not sure who sings that one.
이게 내가 들은 이야기예요.	Okay, then I've got another one for you.

Going Native ~

Another proverb that is a perfect example of how this is used:

콩 심은 데 콩 나고 팥 심은 데 팥 난다. = If you plant beans, beans come up, if you plant red bean, red bean comes up. / You reap what you sow.

---

68) In English we would use progressive tense for the clothes someone 'is wearing' but in Korean, they put them on this morning, so they already 'wore' them.

69) 'Sexy' in Korean is a perfectly fine thing to call someone. The Korean verb is '섹시하다.' This is not to be confused with '야하다' which is closer to the way we use the word 'sexy' in English. '야하다' is much more extreme in its 'sexiness' than '섹시하다.'

70) '만들다' is an irregular 'ㄹ' omission verb. See Section 8.

가 Listen carefully and then circle the correct picture.

4 Answer the question using 'V(으)ㄴ N' and the picture.

1 

어제 친구하고 어디에 갔어요?

→ 어제 ___간___ 곳은 커피숍이었어요.

2 

어제 무슨 책을 읽었어요?

→ 어제 _______ 책은 한국 음악책이었어요.

3 

어제 뭐 먹었어요?

→ 어제 _____________ 것은 초콜릿 아이스크림이었어요.

4 

어제 무슨 영화를 봤어요?

→ 어제 ________ 영화는 슬픈 영화였어요.

5 

생일에 무슨 선물을 받았어요?

→ 생일에 _______ 선물은 시계였어요.

다 **Combine the sentences using 'V(으)ㄴ N.'**

1 어제 커피를 마셨어요. 그 커피는 4,000원이었어요.

<u>   어제 마신 커피는 4,000원이었어요   </u>.

2 주말에 등산했어요. 그 산은 관악산이에요.

_______________________________________.

3 어제 친구를 만났어요. 그 친구는 존이에요.

_______________________________________.

4 지난 금요일에 영화를 봤어요. 그 영화는 재미있었어요.

_______________________________________.

5 어제 신발을 샀어요. 그 신발이 마음에 안 들어요.

_______________________________________.

라 **Read the story and then use 'V(으)ㄴ N' to answer the question.**

어제는 유식이의 생일이었어요. 유식이의 집에서 생일 파티를 했어요. 존도 왔어요. 마이클은 늦게 왔어요. 나는 유식이에게 생일 카드와 CD를 선물로 주었어요. 존은 유식이에게 생일 케이크를 주었어요. 유식이는 맛있는 한국음식을 만들었어요. 생일 파티는 정말 재미있었어요.

1 누가 유식이의 생일에 왔어요?

<u>   유식이의 생일에 온 사람은 나하고 존하고 마이클이에요   </u>.

2 누가 늦게 왔어요?

_______________________________________.

3 나는 유식이한테 무슨 선물을 주었어요?

_______________________________________.

4 존은 유식이한테 무슨 선물을 주었어요?

_______________________________________.

5 유식이는 무슨 음식을 만들었어요?

_______________________________________.

The N(one) that (is) Ving, The N that V

V는 N

| Conjugation | V는 N |

Then there are those times where you are describing a noun that is being effected in some way right now. In that case, you just add '는' on to the end of the verb. Notice that the 받침 enabler '으' vowel is added in the case of past and future tense [(으)ㄴ, (으)ㄹ] but for actions in progress you simply add '는' - no 받침 enabler vowel is ever attached.

텔레비전에 나오는
사람이 누구예요?
Who is that person on television?

한국에 아는 사람이 있어요?
Is there someone who (you) know
in Korea?[71]

나한테 맞는 옷이 많지 않아요.
Not a lot of clothes fit me.

그 여자의 웃는 얼굴이 아주
아름다워요.
Her smiling face is very beautiful.

---

71) 알다 - to know - is an irregular ‘ㄹ’ omission verb. See Chapter 32 for more information.

V는 – 받침less verbs

그건 내가 모르는 단어예요.	Better refer to the dictionary.
우리가 타는 버스가 몇 번이에요?	I may want to ride it again next time.
저기서 자는 아이가 예뻐요.	Take a picture.
지금 하는 숙제가 어려워요.	Ask a Korean for some help.

V는 – verbs with 받침

걷는 운동이 좋아요.	That's why I haven't bought a car.
지금 읽는 책이 재미있어요.	Is that a recommendation?
지금 찾는 것이 뭐예요?	Stop tearing the sofa apart. I'll help you look.

V는 것 – This is one of the favored ways of making a verb into a noun. It's like a gerund or infinitive in English.

먹는 것이 아니에요.	Is it poisonous?
춤을 추는 것이 싫어요.	Take some lessons. You might enjoy it more.
영어를 잘 하는 것이 중요해요.	For traveling and business anyway.
9시간 자는 것은 건강에 안 좋아요.	7 or 8 hours is much better.

Irregular Verbs – ㄹ omission

지금 사는 곳이 어디예요?	Is it near your office?
신문 파는 곳은 어디예요?	I want to pick one up too.
잘 만드는 음식이 뭐예요?	And when are you going to make it for me?

Going Native ~

Koreans are generally a very trusting people, I find, but one of their proverbs cautions against trusting people (or axes) too carelessly.

믿는 도끼에 발등 찍힌다. = The axe you trust will chop your foot.

Skills Building

가 Listen carefully and then circle the correct one.

4 Refer to the story and the following picture and use 'V는 N' to answer the question accordingly.

이 방 안에서 존은 책을 읽고 있어요. 유식이는 사과를 먹고 있어요. 영숙이는 웃고 있어요. 마이클과 미영이는 춤을 추고 있어요. 수잔은 전화를 하고 있어요.

1 누가 존이에요?   책을 읽는 사람이 존이에요   .

2 누가 유식이에요?   ___________________________.

3 누가 영숙이에요?   ___________________________.

4 누가 마이클이에요?   ___________________________.

5 누가 수잔이에요?   ___________________________.

 Change the sentence into the 'V는 N' format.

1 메리는 수영을 잘 해요.   → 수영을 잘 하는 사람이 메리예요.

2 존이 등산을 좋아해요.   → 등산을 ________ 사람이 존이에요.

3 제희가 잘 웃어요,   → 잘 __________ 사람이 제희예요.

4 지금 이태원에 살아요.   → 지금 ________ 곳이 이태원이에요.

5 저기에서 신문을 팔아요.   → 신문을 ________ 곳이 저기예요.

6 비빔밥을 잘 만들어요.   → 잘 ______ 음식이 비빔밥이에요.

 Use 'V는 N' to combine the sentences.

1 영숙이는 여행해요. 그 곳은 제주도예요.

   __영숙이가 여행하는 곳은 제주도예요__________________.

2 유식이는 회사에 다녀요. 그 회사는 우리 집에서 가까워요.

   ______________________________________.

3 존은 여자 친구를 사귀어요. 그 여자는 한국 사람이에요.

   ______________________________________.

4 수잔은 차를 마셔요. 그 차는 녹차예요.

   ______________________________________.

5 마이클 씨는 친구를 만나요. 그 친구는 메리예요.

   ______________________________________.

CHAPTER 24 | The N(one) that will V

V(으)ㄹ N

받침-ending verbs → V을 N

vowel-ending verbs → V ㄹ N

I'm sure that you're getting the idea by now. Of course this one is used to talk about a thing that you're going to do something to or with. It is the future tense version of the last two chapters.

배울 단어가 많아요.
There are lot of words to learn.

그 여자는 만날 남자가 많아요.
That woman has lots of men to meet.

쉴 시간이 없어요.
There's no time to rest.

집에 청소할 게 많아요.[72)]
(I) have a lot of cleaning to do
at home.

---

72) The noun for 'things' or 'stuff' takes many forms. This one is a short form of '것이' where they dropped the 'ㅅ' and pulled over the vowel to make '게.'

V ㄹ

지금 부를 노래가 한국 노래예요.	It's good to know at least one to impress Koreans at the singing room.
내일 볼 공연이 재미있어요.	Everyone's raving about it.
여행할 나라의 돈이 있어요?	Don't arrive penniless.

V 을

신을 등산화를 잊지 마세요.	You gotta have the right shoes.
먹을 것 좀 사서 가요.	Snacks for the trip are important.
받을 편지가 우체국에 있어요.	There's another errand for you.
들을 음악이 없어요.	Time to pick up some CDs.

Here are some very common and useful noun phrases that you'll run a cross a lot:

입을 옷 - something (anything) to wear	*ie.* 입을 옷이 없어요.
먹을 것 - something (anything) to eat	*ie.* 먹을 것이 많아요.
갈 곳 - a place (anywhere) to go	*ie.* 갈 곳이 없어요.
할 일 - something (anything) to do	*ie.* 할 일이 많아요.

And some other key phrases:

V(으)ㄹ 시간이 없어요/있어요.	*ie.* 밥 먹을 시간이 없어요.
V(으)ㄹ 생각이에요.	*ie.* 영화 볼 생각이에요.

Going Native ~

On public transportation you will hear one of these two key expressions all the time:

이번 역의 내리실 문은 오른쪽입니다.[73]

= The exit doors for this station are on the right.

이번 역의 내리실 문은 왼쪽입니다.

= The exit doors for this station are on the reft.

Pay attention and you won't look foolish waiting at the wrong door.

---

73) 내리다 - to get off, to get out of / 오른쪽 - right / 왼쪽 - left

 ## Skills Building

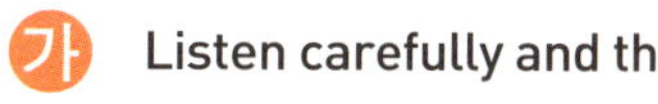 가 **Listen carefully and then circle the correct one.**

1 ㄱ)   ㄴ)   ㄷ)

2 ㄱ)   ㄴ)   ㄷ)

유식   존   유식   영숙   존   영숙

3 ㄱ)   ㄴ)   ㄷ)

4 Use the hint given in the picture and 'V(으)ㄹ N' to rewrite the sentence.

1

친구에게 (주다) 선물은 꽃이에요.

→ ___친구에게 줄 선물은 꽃이에요___.

2

지금 (타다) KTX는 부산에 가요.

→ _______________________.

3

시장에서 (사다) 과일은 사과하고 바나나예요.

→ _______________________.

4

냉장고 안에 (먹다) 것이 없어요.

→ _______________________.

5

우리 가족이 같이 (살다) 집은 큰 집이에요.

→ _______________________.

다 Use 'V(으)ㄹ N' to combine the sentences.

1 영숙이는 여행할 거예요. 그 곳은 제주도예요.

    영숙이가 여행할 곳은 제주도예요 .

2 유식이는 회사에 다닐 거예요. 그 회사는 작은 회사예요.

    _______________________________________ .

3 존은 메리한테 선물을 줄 거예요. 그 선물은 꽃이에요.

    _______________________________________ .

4 수잔은 한국 음식을 만들 거예요. 그 음식은 비빔밥이에요.

    _______________________________________ .

5 마이클은 친구를 만날 거예요. 그 친구는 메리예요.

    _______________________________________ .

라 Make a sentence from the given words using 'V(으)ㄹ N.'

1 듣다, 음악, 없어요.   들을 음악이 없어요 .

2 오늘, 배우다, 단어, 뭐예요?   ______________________ .

3 문, 닫다, 시간이에요.   ______________________ .

4 먹다, 것, 좀 사요.   ______________________ .

5 내리다, 문, 오른쪽입니다.   ______________________ .

6 여행하다, 시간, 없어요.   ______________________ .

Section 7
Showing Respect

Conjugation

받침-ending verbs → V으시

vowel-ending verbs → V시

It's frustrating to the new learner - even when you want to say the exact same thing, you have to learn to say it differently depending on your listener's age, stature, or relationship to you. Granted it's a challenge, but it's also part of what makes learning this language so enjoyable - that you're learning the culture as well. Korean culture is very hierarchical, and being at each stage has its advantages and disadvantages.

You can attach '(으)시' after verbs when talking to other people. It has a 받침 enabler that falls in between when there is a 받침 on the verb. Remember that this is never attached to a verb that refers to yourself! Always use 'V(으)시' to refer to people in generations above your own. Always use it with people who you don't know and seem older than you. Always use it with teachers (another sign of that Confucian tradition of respect for education and educators). Usually use it with people you don't know who are around your age or a little younger. Never use it with children. Nothing makes you sound more like a foreigner than when you use honorific forms with children.

First, some of the proposals:

같이 가시겠어요?
Would (you) like to go with us?

차 한잔하시겠어요?
Would (you) like to have a cup of tea?

And here are some examples of talking about other people's actions:

보 + 시 + 었어요 → 보셨어요
→ 〈웃찾사〉를 보셨어요?[74]
Did (you) see 'Oot-cha-sa?'

읽 + 으시 + ㄹ 거예요 → 읽으실 거예요
→ 아버지께서 신문을 읽으실 거예요.
Father is going to read a newspaper.

---

74) This is one of the most popular programs in Korea. If you spend time with Koreans you'll quickly find that many trendy expressions come from comedy shows like this one. The original title of the show is '웃음을 찾는 사람들' - it's kind of like an acronym.

V(으)시겠어요? – Proposals or Offers

전화하시겠어요?	Or should I give him a ring?
빨간 신발로 하시겠어요?	Or would you like the black pair?
괜찮으시겠어요?	Or would you prefer something else?
전화 지금 받으시겠어요?	Or are you too busy?

V(으)셨어요 – Past tense

전화 잘못 거셨어요.[75]	What number are you trying to reach?
교수님께서 중국에 가셨어요.	Is there a conference?
할머니께서 일을 많이 하셨어요.	She had a long day.
우리 아버지께서 그 책을 읽으셨어요.	But I haven't gotten to it yet.

V(으)실 거예요 – Future tense

삼촌이 월급을 받으실 거예요.	So he's taking us out to dinner next week.
아버지께서 돈이 있으실 거예요.	He'll pay for it when he gets here.
금방 가실 거예요.	It's getting late.
쉬실 거예요?	You deserve a day off.

75) In Korean '잘 못 하다' means 'to not do something well' of course, but when you write the two words together - '잘못 하다' - then the meaning becomes 'to do something wrong' (The verb for 'to input a phone number' is '걸다' - an irregular 'ㄹ' omission verb).

 Listen carefully and then circle the correct picture.

1 ㄱ)   ㄴ)   ㄷ)

2 ㄱ)   ㄴ)   ㄷ)

3 ㄱ) 교수님은 지난 주말에 중국에서 가셨어요.

   ㄴ) 교수님은 어제 중국에 가셨어요.

   ㄷ) 교수님은 이번 주말에 중국에 가실 거예요.

4 Look at the following picture and tell what the family member did using 'V(으)셨어요.'

1

어머니

어머니께서 시장에 가셨어요 .

2

＿＿＿＿＿＿＿＿＿＿＿＿＿＿＿ .

3

아버지

＿＿＿＿＿＿＿＿＿＿＿＿＿＿＿ .

4

＿＿＿＿＿＿＿＿＿＿＿＿＿＿＿ .

5

할아버지

＿＿＿＿＿＿＿＿＿＿＿＿＿＿＿ .

6

＿＿＿＿＿＿＿＿＿＿＿＿＿＿＿ .

다 **Make the following suggestions more polite by adding 'V(으)시.'**

1 (When you invite someone to have a drink)

차 한잔하겠어요? → ___차 한잔하시겠어요___ ?

2 (When you ask your customer if she would like to order)

뭐 주문하겠어요? → ________________ ?

3 (when you ask your friend what movie he wants to see)

무슨 영화 보겠어요? → ________________ ?

4 (When you ask whether your friend wants to ride the bus or the subway)

지하철을 타겠어요? 버스를 타겠어요? → ________________ ?

5 (When you ask your customer what color she wants to buy)

무슨 색을 사겠어요? → ________________ ?

6 (When you ask your classmate where he is going for vacation)

어디에 가겠어요? → ________________ ?

라 **The story in the box tells a little bit about your teacher, Mr. Kim.**
Ask him some questions and then write down what his answers would be.

> 지난 주말에 친구하고 영화를 봤어요. 이번 주에는 등산할 거예요. 유식 씨하고 북
> 한산에 갈 거예요. 아침 9시에 구파발역에서 만날 거예요. 저녁에는 집에서 쉴 거예
> 요. 그리고 한국 잡지를 읽을 거예요.

1 김 선생님은 지난 주말에 뭐 ___하셨어요___ ? 김 선생님: ___친구하고 영화를 봤어요___ .

2 이번 주에는 뭐 ________________ ? 김 선생님: ________________ .

3 어느 산에 ________________ ? 김 선생님: ________________ .

4 유식 씨하고 어디에서 ________________ ? 김 선생님: ________________ .

5 저녁에는 뭐 ________________ ? 김 선생님: ________________ .

6 뭘 ________________ ? 김 선생님: ________________ .

26 V(으)세요, N(이)세요

Conjugation	받침-ending verbs → V으세요 vowel-ending verbs → V세요 받침-ending nouns → N이세요 vowel-ending nouns → N세요

Notice that you weren't taught how to add 'V(으)시' onto the 'V여/아/어요' sentence ending? There's a reason for that; it's not supposed to happen. Although sometimes you will hear a Korean use "V(으)셔요," strictly speaking they are incorrect (I'm not big on speaking strictly, however. Many rural areas in Korea use it frequently and I'd hate to tell them they're wrong). The much more used sentence ending for present tense honorific is 'V(으)세요' as you may have guessed from the title. Also pay attention to the fact that when you are referring to another person as a noun - asking them if they are a teacher, for instance - then you simply add '이세요' after the noun to end the sentence.

There are three main usages of this ending. This is the way to politely tell someone to do something. It's the imperative (command) ending that is the equivalent of adding 'Please ~.' Next it is used as a polite present tense interrogative (question) ending. And finally it is used for declarative (statement) sentences referring to someone else's actions - in the same way as 'V(으)시.'

Imperative:

숙제를 꼭 하세요.
Make sure to do (your) homework.[76]

---

76) '꼭' is usually translated to 'definitely' but often it's closer to 'make sure to V.'

책 많이 읽으세요.
Read lots of books.

Interrogative:

선생님이세요?
Are (you) a teacher?

매일 운동하세요?
Do (you) exercise everyday?

Declarative:

아버지께서 매일 신문을 보세요.
(My) father looks at the paper
every day.

우리 언니는 치마를 자주 입으세요.
My older sister wears skirts often.

명령형(Imperatives)

안녕히 가세요.[77]	I'm staying. Or maybe I'm of somewhere too.
전화 좀 받으세요.	It's for you.
쉬세요.	You look tired. Take a load off.

부정 명령형(Negative Imperatives)

늦지 마세요.	Three times equals one absence.
가지 마세요.	The fun's just getting started.
치마를 입지 마세요.	I don't want men checking out your legs.

의문형(Interrogatives)

안녕하세요?[78]	Yes. And yourself?
바쁘세요?	Can you take a call?
추우세요?[79]	Would you like me to close the window?

평서형(Declaratives)

그 의사 선생님이 멋있으세요.	That explains all those female patients.
할머니께서 지금 청소하세요.	She should rest more at her age.
현욱 씨는 자주 웃으세요.	He must have a good sense of humor.

N(이)세요?

몇 살이세요?	If you don't mind me asking.
처음이세요?	Or have you tried this before?
의사세요?	Could you take a look at this mole?

Going Native ~

The heart and mind are very important to Koreans - so you can ask how they feel about something by asking about how it appeals to their heart.

마음에 드세요?[80] = Do you like it?   마음에 안 드세요? = You don't like it?

---

77) Have you used this way of saying goodbye yet? You've been telling people to "Go peacefully." '안녕' is peace, and '히' makes it into an adverb.

78) Remember it's always a question, even if the intonation may not seem like it. Your answer should be "네." and then you ask them back - "안녕하세요?"

79) See Section 8 - 'ㅂ' irregular.

80) '들다' - to be appealing to - is a 'ㄹ' omission irregular verb. See Section 8.

Skills Building

가 Listen carefully and then circle the correct one.

1   ㄱ)   ㄴ)   ㄷ)

2   ㄱ) 존 씨는 매일 운동해요.

    ㄴ) 존 씨는 주말에 집에서 쉬어요.

    ㄷ) 존 씨는 집 근처에서 운동해요.

3   ㄱ) 유식 씨는 메리 씨를 만날 거예요.

    ㄴ) 메리 씨는 친구를 만날 거예요.

    ㄷ) 유식 씨는 커피숍에 갈 거예요.

4 Look at the following picture and use 'V(으)세요' to complete the sentences.

1 

선생님께서 <u>한국어를 가르치세요</u>.

2 

어머니께서 ___________________.

3 

아버지께서 ___________________.

4 

할아버지께서 ___________________.

5 

어머니께서 ___________________.

6 

아버지께서 ___________________.

다 **유식** is on his first **미팅**(blind date). He must be careful to be very polite, so change his questions into a more polite form using 'V(으)시' or 'V(으)세요.'

1 커피 한잔하겠어요? ___커피 한잔하시겠어요___ ?

2 지금 무슨 일을 해요? ______________ ?

3 요즘 회사일이 많아요? ______________ ?

4 무슨 음식을 좋아해요? ______________ ?

5 지난 휴가에 뭐 했어요? ______________ ?

6 의사 선생님이에요? ______________ ?

라 Change the following into positive and negative commands.

1 전화합니다. ___전화하세요___ . – ___전화하지 마세요___ .

2 기다립니다. ______________ . – ______________ .

3 운동합니다. ______________ . – ______________ .

4 웃습니다. ______________ . – ______________ .

5 집에 갑니다. ______________ . – ______________ .

6 책을 읽습니다. ______________ . – ______________ .

27 Honorific Vocabulary

Vocabulary Modifications

Markers:	이/가 → 께서	에게 → 께	
Nouns:	집 → 댁	나이 → 연세	
	이름 → 성함	밥 (음식) → 진지	
	명 → 분	생일 → 생신	

Usage

Discussing a person's behavior towards superiors:

P에게 주다 → P께 드리다

P에게 말하다 → P께 말씀을 드리다

Discussing a superior's behavior:

말하다 → 말씀을 하시다   먹다 → 드시다, 잡수시다

자다 → 주무시다   있다 → 계시다[81]

The final key to impressing Koreans with your consideration is perhaps the hardest. Once again, people rarely expect you to do it and will be very impressed if you do. Memorize the words above and then listen for them when you are listening to other Koreans talking first.

The first thing to pay attention to is that some of the roots of the verbs end in '시,' so you don't have to bother adding on another '시' to the end of these verbs.

Here's how you talk to a superior with these:

많이 드세요.
Bon appetite![82]

---

81) This applies only to the 'to exist' meaning of '있다.' For 'to have' - showing possession or ownership - leave it as '있다' and add '세요.' ending to be polite - ie. "돈이 있으세요?"

82) In Korea this is a very common invitation to enjoy your meal. Don't worry, you don't have to eat too much.

피곤하세요? 주무세요.
Are (you) tired? Sleep.

Here's how you talk about a superior with these:

할머니께서 진지를 드셨어요.
Grandma ate her food.

교수님 계세요?[83]
Is the professor here?

Here's how you talk about yourself:

저는 교수님께 말씀을 드렸어요.
(I) told the professor.

---

83) When you use the '계시다' in a sentence instead of '있다,' often the subject marker is omitted.

Talking to superiors[84]

진지 드셨어요?	Or should we grab something now?
학교에 계셨어요?	What time did you leave?
선생님 댁이 어디세요?	Is it nearby?
푹 주무세요.[85]	You look tired.

Talking about superiors

할머니께서 주무세요.	Don't make too much noise.
할아버지께서 말씀하셨어요.	Then you'd better do it.
아버지께서 아직 진지를 드시지 않았어요.	Maybe we should wait for him.
어머니께서 집에 안 계세요.	When will she be back?

Talking about yourself and your superiors

그분께 말씀을 드렸어요.	So they already know.
선생님 댁에 갔어요.	I wasn't invited!
할아버지 연세가 많지 않으세요?	He's young to be a grandfather.

N이/가 어떻게 되세요? – What/How is N constituted?

성함이 어떻게 되세요?	I'm Stephen.
연세가 어떻게 되세요?	You look much younger.
가족이 어떻게 되세요?	Are you married?

Going Native ~

When your parents are headed to bed you can say:

안녕히 주무세요 = Sleep well. (For your friend, it's '잘자')

---

84) 'Superior' is a slightly derogatory term in English. Please don't think of it that way. It just means that they've earned their stripes - either by way of their age or education they have earned the respect you should show your seniors.

85) '푹' is an adverb used almost exclusively with verbs related to resting - ie. '푹 쉬다, 푹 자다.'

가 Listen carefully and then circle the correct one.

1 ㄱ) 김 선생님께서 유식이에게 전화하셨어요.

ㄴ) 김 선생님께서 학교에 계세요.

ㄷ) 유식이가 학교에 없어요.

2 ㄱ) 김 선생님은 점심을 안 드실 거예요.

ㄴ) 김 선생님은 이 선생님하고 같이 점심을 드실 거예요.

ㄷ) 이 선생님은 점심을 안 드셨어요.

3 ㄱ) 할아버지하고 할머니께서 댁에 계세요.

ㄴ) 할아버지께서 지금 주무세요.

ㄷ) 할머니께서 댁에 계세요.

나 Look at the following pictures and complete the sentences accordingly.

1

선생님께서 __교실에 계세요__________.

2

아버지께서 _____________________.

3

할아버지께 _____________________.

4

할머니 _____________________.

5

어머니께서 _____________________.

6

할아버지 _____________________.

 What should you say in these situations?

1 When your parents are headed to bed

→ _안녕히 주무세요_ .

2 Before eating → _____________________!

3 When you want to know your doctor's name

→ _____________________?

4 When you ask someone who is much older what her name is

→ _____________________?

5 When you are leaving your teacher's office

→ _____________________.

6 When you bump into your teacher around lunch time

→ _____________________?

라 **Change the underlines more polite.**

1 1월 1일에 우리는 교수님 집에 갔어요.

1월 1일에 우리는 교수님 댁에 갔어요 .

2 교수님이 우리를 초대했어요.

_____________________.

3 우리는 교수님한테 줄 꽃을 샀어요.

_____________________.

4 우리는 교수님한테 꽃을 주었어요.

_____________________.

5 교수님이 "꽃이 아주 예뻐요"라고 말했어요.

_____________________.

6 우리는 교수님한테 "새해 복 많이 받으세요"라고 말했어요.

_____________________.

Section 8
Irregular Verbs

28 ' ㅂ ' Irregular Verbs

Conjugation — When ' ㅂ ' irregular verbs meet a vowel, the ' ㅂ ' changes to an 우:
irregular A/V ' ㅂ ' 받침 + vowel = 우

When irregular verbs or adjectives ending in a ' ㅂ ' 받침 meet up with a vowel, then the ' ㅂ ' changes to an ' 우.' But be careful! Not all adjectives and verbs that end in ' ㅂ ' are irregular verbs! Some, like ' 입다 '(to wear) are regular verbs - ' 입어요.' When you're not sure and you have to make a guess, chances are that the adjectives are irregular verbs and the verbs are regular. But of course since this doesn't always hold true, you'll have to keep studying and listening until you've memorized them all.

And one more tip: for conjunctions and sentence endings that have a 받침 enabler ' 으 ' before them, like ' (으)세요 ', you have to change the ' 으 ' to ' 우 ' as well.

맵＋어요: 매ㅜ＋어요
(ㅂ → ㅜ)　　(ㅜ＋어)
→ 매워요. (It's) spicy.

어렵＋어요: 어려ㅜ＋어요
(ㅂ → ㅜ)　　(ㅜ＋어)

→ 어려워요. (This is) difficult.

Extension

Vㅂ

침대에 누워요.86)	The doctor will be in to see you in a moment.
도와주세요.87)	I'll be with you in one minute.

Aㅂ

나는 사장님이 미워요.88)	Really? I thought you got along well?
추우세요?89)	I'll turn up the heater.
한국말이 쉬워요.	You can't disagree with this one enough, can you?
가까워요?	It's not too far.
국이 싱거워요.	Add some salt and pepper.

---

86) '눕다' and '돕다' - to lie down, (especially on your back) and to help - are the only irregular verbs of this form you are likely to run into. The rest will be adjectives.

87) '돕다' is the verb for 'to help'. But when you do something for someone '아/어주다' is attached on to the end of the verb and since 'help' is always for someone else this helping verb is almost always attached to '돕다'. This sentence is asking for some help.

88) Pay attention to the markers here. I hate him is "나는 그 남자가 미워요." And yes - to hate is an adjective in Korean. That's why the subject marker is attached to the person who is being hated and the contrastive/topic marker is attached to the person who is hating.

89) This is that example I warned you about in the beginning. The sentence ending is '(으)세요' but in the case of transforming 'ㅂ' verbs, the resulting '우' is used instead of the 받침 enabler '으.'

201

Again, the big challenge is that not all verbs ending in '㉠' 받침 are irregular. The majority of verbs ending in a '㉠' 받침 (ie. 받다, 닫다, 믿다 etc.) are actually regular verbs that you don't have to worry about. However there are three common crucial '㉠'받침 transforming irregular verbs that all beginners must learn. The key verbs to know are '듣다' (to listen), '걷다' (to walk), '묻다' (to ask).

잘 들으세요.
Listen carefully.
(Literally, "Listen well.")

우리가 많이 걸었어요.
We walked a lot.

Extension

못 들었어요.	Okay. I'll talk louder.
친구한테 물어보세요.90)	I'll give you an answer.
그 여자 이름을 물었어요?	What about her phone number?
매일 집까지 걸어요.	It's not too far.
들으셨어요?	There's big news!

---

90) Most of the time people don't say '물어요' but '물어봐요' Adding '아/어보다' on to the end of verbs is like adding 'try Ving' to the verb - so they're usually saying something closer to 'Try asking ~.'

30 '르' Irregular Verbs

Conjugation

A/V ending in 르 when conjugated into the 아/어 form:
① the '—' vowel is dropped ② the '르' is doubled ③ 아 or 어 is added according to the vowel from the previous syllable (오/아 + 아/all other vowels + 어).

If you read the conjugation first you are probably left thoroughly confused. Here's how it works.

모르다 → 모ㄹ → 몰ㄹ → 몰라요
　　　　　① 　　② 　　③

An example clears things up a bit, doesn't it? The good news is that if an adjective/verb ends in the syllable '르' then it is guaranteed to be an irregular '르.' It's not like the previous irregulars, when some verbs are and some aren't. All verbs ending '르' are irregular. And there's really only five A/V that a beginner is likely to run into:

Verbs　　　모르다 (to not know), 고르다 (to choose), 부르다 (to sing or call out)

Adjectives　다르다 (to be different), 빠르다 (to be fast)

Track 86

값이 달라요.
The price is different.

하나 골라요.
Pick one.

Extension

지하철이 더 빨라요.	Don't bother driving.
노래를 불렀어요.	Now it's your turn.
몰랐어요.	I'm glad you finally told me.

And when you don't know a thing about the topic there's a great expression you can use:

하나도 몰라요. = I don't know anything about that.

31 '으' Irregular Verbs

Conjugation

When A/V ending in the vowel 으 are conjugated into the 아/어 form: ① Drop the '一' ② Add 아 or 어 according to the vowel of the first syllable.

Here's the example:

아프다 → 아ㅍ → 아파요
　　　　　①　　　②

This one is even easier, isn't it? There is one exception, but then you may have figured that one out already. It's verbs that end in the syllable '르.' In those cases you follow the rules presented for the previous irregular verb. For all the others, use this method:

Verbs	쓰다 (to write)
Adjectives	고프다 (to be hungry or wanting), 바쁘다 (to be busy), 슬프다 (to be sad), 아프다 (to be in pain), 예쁘다 (to be pretty), 크다 (to be big)

그 영화가 아주 슬퍼요.
That movie's really sad.

Extension

자주 편지를 써요.	Your girlfriend must appreciate that.
배가 고파요.	Then let's get something to eat.
저 여자가 예뻐요.	She'll be popular with the men.
우리 형이 아주 바빠요.	It must be tough to see him.

---

91) As a single syllable verb, there is no previous syllable vowel to use to decide, so you go to the default '어' making it '커요.' The single syllable '쓰다' works the same way.

32 '르' Omission Irregular Verbs

Conjugation   For all verbs or adjectives ending in '르', the '르' is always dropped when the A/V is attached to the consonants '니', '비', or '시'.

Another habit to form, but once again it holds true for all verbs that end in a '르' 받침 so you don't have to memorize which verbs it applies to and which it doesn't. The challenge is that it only applies when it bumps up with one of the three consonants above. The good news is that there are only a few conjunctions, sentence endings or auxiliaries that this will happen frequently with. Another thing to remember is that for these verbs often the '으' or '이' 받침 enablers are omitted because the '르' is dropped ahead of time, so there is no '르' 받침 to pronounce:

Verbs   알다 (to know), 울다 (to cry), 살다 (to live), 놀다 (to play or hang out), 만들다 (to make), 날다 (to fly), 밀다 (to push)

Adjectives   길다 (to be long), 멀다 (to be far), 달다 (to be sweet)

Conjunctions/Sentence Endings

(으)받침 enabler omission   **A/V세요**

예) 만들다 : 만들 + 세요 → 만드세요

Auxiliary

A/V시

예) 만들다 : 만들 + 실 거예요 → 만드실 거예요

(으)받침 enabler omission   **A니 N**

예) 길다 : 길 + 니 → 긴 (머리)

V는 N

예) 만들다 : 만들 + 니 → 만든 (음식)

아는 사람이에요?
Do (you) know this person?

어디에 사세요?
Where do (you) live?

ㄹ Omission Irregular Verbs

우는 사람이 누구예요?	What happened to make her do that?
내가 사는 동네가 조용해요.	You must sleep well at night.
재미있게 노세요.	But not too much fun.

ㄹ Omission Irregular Adjectives

먼 곳에 갔어요.	Did she go abroad?
단 음식이 싫어요.	Would you like black coffee then?
머리가 긴 여자가 아름다워요.	I prefer short hair myself.

Skills Building

가 Listen carefully and then circle the correct one.

1 ㄱ)   ㄴ)   ㄷ)

2 ㄱ) 누나는 머리가 길어요.

ㄴ) 누나는 키가 커요.

ㄷ) 누나는 바빠요.

3 ㄱ) 영숙이는 여의도에 살아요.

ㄴ) 영숙이는 여의도역까지 걸어요.

ㄷ) 존은 이태원역에서 먼 곳에 살아요.

4 Look at the following picture and make a sentence using the verb given.

1

(모르다) ___잘 몰라요___ .

2

(아프다) _______________ .

3

(쓰다) _______________ .

4

(부르다) _______________ .

5

(맵다) _______________ .

6

(고프다) _______________ .

7

(듣다) _______________ .

8

(덥다) _______________ .

다 **Correct the following adjectives/verbs.**

1 저기 (울다)는 아이가 누구예요?   우는

2 저는 (달다)ㄴ/은 음식을 좋아해요.

3 제가 (만들다)ㄴ/은 김치예요.

4 저는 머리가 (길다)ㄴ/은 여자가 좋아요.

5 어디에 (살다)(으)세요?

6 저 사람은 (알다)는 사람이에요.

라 **Correct the underlined mistakes.**

1 어제 집에서 학교까지 걷었어요.   걸었어요 .

2 한국말이 어렵어요.   .

3 좋아하는 색을 고라요.   .

4 문을 밀세요.   .

5 우리 형이 키가 크요.   .

6 일본말을 모라요.   .

7 우리 누나가 아주 바쁘요.   .

8 친구가 멀은 곳에 살아요.   .

Appendix

- **Extension** English Translation
- **Skills Building** Answer Key
- **Basic Verb/Adjective** Conjugations

Extension English Translation

▶▶Section 1

Chapter 1

오늘 며칠이에요?	▸▸ What is the date today?
학생이에요.	▸▸ I'm a student.
스무살이에요.	▸▸ I'm 20 years old.
우리 집이에요.	▸▸ This is my house.
어디예요?	▸▸ Where is it? Where am I?
이게 한국말로 뭐예요?	▸▸ What is this in Korean?
얼마예요?	▸▸ How much is it?
어느 나라 사람이에요?	▸▸ What country are you from? / What country person are you?
미국 사람이 아니에요.	▸▸ I'm not American.
책이 아니에요.	▸▸ It's/That's not a book.
텔레비전이 아니에요.	▸▸ It's/That's not a television.
언니가 아니에요. 동생이에요.	▸▸ She's/That's not my older sister. She's my younger sibling.
콜라가 아니에요. 사이다예요.	▸▸ It's/That's not a cola. It's a lemon-lime soda.
소주가 아니에요. 물이에요.	▸▸ It's/That's not soju. It's water.

Chapter 2

뭐 해요?	▸▸ What are you doing?
심심해요?	▸▸ Are you bored?
어디에서 공부해요?	▸▸ Where do you study?
미안해요.	▸▸ I'm sorry.
작아요.	▸▸ It's/That's small.
아주 좋아요.	▸▸ It's/That's very good.
매일 가요.	▸▸ I go everyday.

언제 와요?   ›› When is she/he coming?

밥을 먹어요.   ›› Have some food. / Have a meal.

주말에 쉬어요?   ›› Do you rest on the weekend? / Do you have the weekend off?

뭘 배워요?   ›› What are you learning?

음악을 들어요.   ›› Listen to the music.

잘 지내요?   ›› How are you?

선배가 돈을 내요.   ›› The seniors treat us.

Chapter 3

어제 전화했어요.   ›› I called yesterday.

심심했어요.   ›› I was bored.

어제 뭐 했어요?   ›› What did you do yesterday?

그 책이 좋았어요.   ›› That's a good book.

서울에서 살았어요.   ›› I live in Seoul.

지갑을 찾았어요.   ›› I found my wallet.

밥을 먹었어요?   ›› Did you eat?

예뻤어요.   ›› She/He/It was pretty.

1시간 기다렸어요.   ›› I waited an hour.

오빠가 집에 왔어요?   ›› Did my brother come home?

비디오를 봤어요.   ›› I saw a video.

어제 밤 10시에 잤어요.   ›› I slept last night at 10 o'clock.

어디 갔어요?   ›› Where did you/she/he go?

일본어 배웠어요.   ›› I learned Japanese.

십만 원을 줬어요.   ›› I gave her/him a hundred thousand won.

Chapter 4

그 영화가 재미있을 거예요.   ›› That movie will be good.

숙제가 어려울 거예요.   ›› The homework is going to be difficult.

내일 피곤할 거예요.   ›› I'm/You're going to be tired tomorrow.

김치가 매울 거예요.   ›› That kimchi is going to be spicy.

아마 누나가 집에 없을 거예요.   ›› My older sister probably won't be home.

아마 슈퍼에 토마토가 있을 거예요.   ›› There probably won't be any tomatoes at the market.

아마 선생님은 아이가 있을 거예요. ▸▸ The teacher probably has children.
일요일이에요. 아마 일이 없을 거예요. ▸▸ It's Sunday. She/He won't have work today.
아침을 먹을 거예요. ▸▸ I'm/She's/He's/You're going to have breakfast.
편지를 쓸 거예요. ▸▸ I'm/She's/He's/You're going to write a letter.
집에 갈 거예요. ▸▸ I'm/She's/He's/You're going to go home.
술을 마실 거예요. ▸▸ I'm/She's/He's/You're going to drink alcohol.
힘들지 않을 거예요. ▸▸ It won't be too hard.
안 추울 거예요. ▸▸ It won't be cold.
안 비쌀 거예요. ▸▸ It won't be expensive.
너무 복잡하지 않을 거예요. ▸▸ It won't be too crowded.

Chapter 5

따뜻하겠습니다. ▸▸ It'll be warm.
덥겠습니다. ▸▸ It'll be hot.
눈이 오겠습니다. ▸▸ It's going to snow.
춥겠습니다. ▸▸ It's going to be cold.
이거 사시겠어요? ▸▸ Would you like to buy this?
영화표를 예매하시겠어요? ▸▸ Would you like to reserve a ticket?
그것 좀 주시겠어요? ▸▸ Could you give me that, please?
기다리시겠어요? ▸▸ Could you wait, please?
도와주시겠어요? ▸▸ Would you assist me please?
모르겠어요. ▸▸ I don't know. / I'm not sure.
알겠어요. ▸▸ I see. / I understand.
처음 뵙겠습니다. ▸▸ Nice to meet you.

Chapter 6

한국말을 배우고 있어요. ▸▸ I'm learning Korean.
약을 먹고 있어요. ▸▸ I'm taking medicine.
일하고 있어요. ▸▸ I'm working.
빨간 셔츠를 입고 있어요. ▸▸ She/He is wearing a red shirt.
운전하고 계세요. ▸▸ She/He is driving.
신문을 읽고 계세요. ▸▸ She/He is reading the paper.
아빠가 일하고 계세요. ▸▸ Dad is working.

엄마가 뭐하고 계세요?   ▶▶ What is mom doing?
어제 7시에 밥을 먹고 있었어요. ▶▶ I was eating at 7 o'clock yesterday.
지하철 타고 있었어요. ▶▶ I was riding the subway.
형이 공부하고 있었어요. ▶▶ My older brother was studying.
검은색을 찾고 있었어요. ▶▶ I was looking for a black one.

Chapter 7

준식이는 돈이 있어요. ▶▶ Jun-shik has money.
진희는 돈이 없어요. ▶▶ Jin-hee doesn't have money.
제희는 돈이 많이 있어요. ▶▶ Jae-hee has a lot of money.
성수는 숙제가 없어요. ▶▶ Song-soo doesn't have homework.
주희는 숙제가 있어요. ▶▶ Joo-hee has homework.
재훈이는 숙제가 없어요. ▶▶ Jae-hoon doesn't have homework.
책이 편의점에 있어요. ▶▶ The book is at the convenience store.
책이 도서관에 많이 있어요. ▶▶ The book is at the library.
책이 커피숍에 없어요. ▶▶ The book isn't at the coffee shop.
성수가 학교에 없어요. ▶▶ Song-soo is not at school.
지원이가 학교에 없어요. ▶▶ Ji-won is not at school.
은숙이가 학교에 있어요. ▶▶ Eun-sook is at school.

▶▶Section 2

Chapter 8

비행기가 아직 안 왔어요. ▶▶ The plane isn't here yet.
버스를 안 타요. 기차를 타요. ▶▶ I'm/We're not riding a bus. We're riding the train.

오늘 술 안 마셔요. ▶▶ I'm not drinking tonight.
안 추워요? ▶▶ Aren't you cold?
키가 안 커요. ▶▶ I'm/She's/He's not tall.
안 무거워요. ▶▶ It's not heavy.
왜 전화 안 했어요? ▶▶ Why didn't you call?
운동 안 해요. ▶▶ I don't/She doesn't/He doesn't exercise.

요리 안 할 거예요.   ▸▸ I'm not going to cook.
비행기가 도착했어요?   ▸▸ Did the plane arrive yet?
폴이 왔어요?   ▸▸ Did Paul arrive?
전화했어요?   ▸▸ Did she/he call?

Chapter 9

열심히 일하지 않아요.   ▸▸ She/He doesn't work hard.
담배를 피우지 않아요.   ▸▸ I don't/She doesn't/He doesn't smoke.
딸기를 먹지 않아요.   ▸▸ I don't/She doesn't/He doesn't eat strawberries.
선생님 말씀을 듣지 않아요?   ▸▸ Aren't you listening to what the teacher is saying?

가볍지 않아요.   ▸▸ It's not light.
아름답지 않아요.   ▸▸ It's not beautiful.
바쁘지 않아요.   ▸▸ I'm not busy.
많지 않아요.   ▸▸ There aren't many.
어제 학교에 가지 않았어요.   ▸▸ I didn't go to school yesterday.
수업 시간에 심심하지 않았어요?   ▸▸ Weren't you tired in class?
돈을 주지 않았어요.   ▸▸ You didn't give me money.
파티에 오지 않았어요.   ▸▸ She didn't come to the party.
비싸지 않을 거예요.   ▸▸ It won't be expensive.
쉽지 않을 거예요.   ▸▸ It won't be easy.
유식이가 보내지 않을 거예요.   ▸▸ Yoo-sik won't send it.
메리가 파티에 가지 않을 거예요.   ▸▸ Mary doesn't go to the party.

Chapter 10

늦지 마세요.   ▸▸ Don't be late.
담배를 피우지 마세요.   ▸▸ Don't smoke.
술을 마시지 마세요.   ▸▸ Don't drink.
집에 가지 마세요.   ▸▸ Don't go home.
너무 비싸요. 사지 마세요.   ▸▸ It's too expensive. Don't buy it.
말하지 마.   ▸▸ Don't speak.
아직 자지 마.   ▸▸ Don't sleep yet.

돈을 주지 마.   » Don't give me money.
버스를 타지 마.   » Don't ride the bus.
기다리지 마.   » Don't wait.
걱정 마.   » Don't worry.

»Section 3

Chapter 11

형이 나갔어요.   » My older brother went out.
음악이 너무 빨라요.   » The music is too fast.
신발이 예뻐요.   » The shoes are pretty.
이게 뭐예요?   » What is this?
친구가 기다려요.   » My friend is waiting.
나무가 많아요.   » There are a lot of trees.
날씨가 따뜻해요.   » The weather is warm.
민주가 지금 자요.   » Min-joo is sleeping.
제가 쇼핑할게요!   » I'll do the shopping!
정호 씨가 전화할 거예요. » Jung-ho is going to call.
제가 청소할게요!   » I'll do the cleaning!
누가 스티븐이에요?   » Who is Stephen?
제가 스티븐이에요.   » I'm Stephen.

Chapter 12

한국말을 공부해요.   » I study Korean.
약을 먹었어요.   » I took medicine.
수업을 잘 들어요.   » Listen carefully to the class.
편의점을 찾고 있어요. » I'm looking for a convenience store.
녹차를 마셔요.   » Drink green tea.
반바지를 입어요.   » Wear shorts.
철수가 미영이를 만났어요. » Chul-soo met Min-young.
일요일에 축구를 할 거예요. » I'm going to play soccer on Sunday.

편지를 받았어요.   »» I got a letter.
소풍을 갈 거예요.   »» We're going on a picnic.
6시간을 자요.   »» I sleep six hours (a night).
음악을 들을 거예요.   »» I 'm going to listen to music.
어딜 가요?   »» Where are you going?
뭘 해요?   »» What are you doing?
누굴 기다려요?   »» Whom are you waiting for?
뭘 먹었어요?   »» What are you eating?

Chapter 13

지원 씨는 고기를 안 먹어요.   »» Ji-won doesn't eat meat.
어제 숙제는 아주 어려웠어요.   »» The homework yesterday was very difficult.
우리 형은 대학생이에요.   »» My older brother is a college student.
이 식당은 아주 맛있어요.   »» This restaurant is delicious.
밥은 먹을 거예요.   »» I'm going to eat.
음악은 안 들려요.   »» I don't hear the music.
가게는 못 봤어요.   »» I didn't see the store.
책은 많이 읽었어요.   »» I read a lot of books.
처음에는 김치를 못 먹었어요.   »» I couldn't eat kimchi at first.
편의점에선 안 팔아요.   »» They don't sell it at convenience stores.
대전까지는 KTX로 가요.   »» Go to Taejeon by KTX.
동생에게는 안 보냈어요.   »» I didn't send it to my brother.
한국말이 나한테는 어려워요.   »» Korean is very difficult for me.

»»Section 4

Chapter 14

백화점이랑 슈퍼마켓이 있어요.   »» There is a department store and a supermarket.
이름이랑 나이를 쓰세요.   »» Write your name and age.
가격이랑 디자인이 정말 괜찮아요. »» The price and design are pretty good.
      (lit: really okay)
동생이랑 동생의 남자친구가   »» My younger sister and her boyfriend came to

집에 왔어요. — our house.

전화하고 침대를 샀어요. — I bought a phone and a bed.

간호사하고 의사가 아주 좋아요. — The nurse and doctor are very good.

상추하고 삼겹살을 주세요. — Give me lettuce and pork please.

아침하고 저녁에 약을 드세요. — Take the medicine in the morning and at night.

한국과 일본은 가까워요. — Korea and Japan are close.

은행은 서점과 우체국 사이에 있어요. — It's between the book store and the post office.

러시아와 중국을 여행할 거예요. — I'm going on a trip to Russia and China.

봄과 가을에 날씨가 좋아요. — The weather is nice in spring and fall.

여자 친구하고 싸웠어요. — I fought with my girlfriend.

그 사람하고 가세요. — Go with your friend.

택시 기사랑 이야기 많이 했어요. — I talked a lot with the taxi driver.

한국 친구랑 사귀었어요. — I made a Korean friend.

Chapter 15

노트북이나 PC를 살까요? — Should I buy a notebook or a PC?

화요일이나 수요일에 할 거예요. — They will do it on Tuesday or Wednesday.

술이나 담배 많이 하면 안 좋아요. — It's not good if you drink or smoke too much.

중국이나 싱가포르를 여행할 거예요. — I am going to travel to China or Singapore.

노란색이나 빨간색이 있어요. — We have yellow or red.

서강대나 서울대에서 한국어를 공부할 거예요. — I'm going to study at Sogang University or Seoul National University.

주말에는 비디오나 디비디를 봐요. — I watch a video or DVD on the weekends.

저녁에 숙제나 운동을 해요. — I do homework or exercise at night.

이메일이나 팩스로 보내세요. — Send an email or fax, please.

주말에 등산이나 갈 거예요. — I'm going to go hiking or something on the weekend.

밥이나 먹을까요? — Shall we eat or something?

방학에 영어공부나 할 거예요. — I'm going to study or something over the vacation.

영화나 볼까요? — Should we see a movie or something?

존 씨의 여자 친구도 왔어요.	≫ John's girlfriend came too.
아침하고 저녁에도 운동해요.	≫ I exercise in the morning and night.
넥타이도 사세요.	≫ Buy a necktie too.
노래하고 춤도 출 거예요.	≫ I'm going to sing and dance.
명동에도 갈 거예요.	≫ We're going to go to Myung-dong.
민주도 안 해요.	≫ Min-joo isn't going to do it either.
나도 숙제하지 않았어요.	≫ I didn't do the homework either.
우리 언니도 돈이 없어요.	≫ My older sister doesn't have any money either.
학교에도 그 책이 없어요.	≫ They don't have that book at school either.
회사에도 안 가요.	≫ I'm not even going to work.
나는 돈이 10원도 없어요.	≫ I don't even have 10 won.
한 번도 안 갔어요.	≫ I haven't even gone once.
하나도 몰라요.	≫ I don't know anything about it.

컴퓨터의 문제가 뭐예요?	≫ What is wrong with the computer.
재운이의 여자 친구가 일본 사람이에요.	≫ Jae-woon's girlfriend is Japanese.
대구의 사과가 제일 맛있어요.	≫ Taegu apples are the tastiest.
한국의 음식이 맛있어요.	≫ Korean food is delicious.
그 사람은 누구 오빠예요?	≫ Whose brother is that?
선영 씨 오빠예요.	≫ That's Sun-young's brother.
이게 유식이 오토바이예요.	≫ This is Yoo-shik's motorcycle.
이 방은 동생 방이에요.	≫ This room is my younger sibling's room.
제 이름은 제임스예요.	≫ My name is James.
제 형이 회사원이에요.	≫ My older brother is a businessman.
내 거예요.	≫ I'll pay.
내 일이 아직 안 끝났어요.	≫ My work isn't finished.

Chapter 18

친구에게 물어보세요.	▸▸ Ask a friend.
나한테 거짓말을 하지 마세요.	▸▸ Don't lie to me.
친구에게 말을 할까요?	▸▸ Should I tell a friend?
선생님께 말씀을 드려요.	▸▸ Tell the teacher please.
그 사진이 누구한테 있어요?	▸▸ Who has that picture?
지금 저에게 없어요.	▸▸ I don't have it right now.
열쇠가 언니한테 있어요.	▸▸ My older sister has the key.
제 휴대전화가 선생님께 있어요.	▸▸ My teacher has my cell phone.
저한테 기회를 주세요.	▸▸ Please give me a chance.
동생한테 정말 미안해요.	▸▸ I'm really sorry to my younger sibling.
외국 사람에게 한국어를 가르쳐요.	▸▸ I teach foreigners Korean.
우리 딸에게 그 일을 시켰어요.	▸▸ I had my daughter do that work.
그 가게는 손님에게 친절해요.	▸▸ That restaurant is very kind to customers.
그 음식이 여자에게 안 좋아요.	▸▸ That food is not good for women.
한국말이 외국인에게 어려워요.	▸▸ Korean is difficult to foreigners.
우리 가족한테 보내요.	▸▸ Send it to my family.

Chapter 19

명동에 사람들이 많아요.	▸▸ There are a lot of people in Myung-dong.
명숙이가 편의점에 갔어요.	▸▸ Myung-sook went to a convenience store.
그 호텔이 용산구에 있어요.	▸▸ That hotel is in Yongsan-gu.
아침 일곱 시에 학교에 가요.	▸▸ I go to school at 7 A.M.
영화가 여섯 시에 시작할 거예요.	▸▸ The movie is going to start at 6 o'clock.
여름에 비가 많이 와요.	▸▸ It rains a lot in the summer.
담배가 건강에 나빠요.	▸▸ Cigarettes are bad for your health.
당근이 눈에 좋아요.	▸▸ Carrots are good for your eyes.
삼계탕이 몸에 좋아요.	▸▸ Samgaetang is good for health. (lit: body)
신촌에서 만나요.	▸▸ Let's meet in Shinchon.
회사에서 일해요.	▸▸ I work at a company.

집에서 쉬었어요.   » I rest at home.
어디에서 왔어요?   » Where are you from? (lit: Where did you come from?)

베트남에서 왔어요.   » I'm from Vietnam.
집에서 학교까지 30분 걸려요.   » From my house to school it takes 30 minutes.

Chapter 20

버스로 왔어요.   » We came by bus.
자동차로 회사에 다녀요.   » I commute to work by car.
기차로 갈 거예요.   » We're going by train.
자전거로 학교에 다녀요.   » I go to school by bicycle.
영어로 말해요.   » (Let's) talk in English.
디카로 사진 찍었어요.   » Take a picture with a digital camera.
인터넷으로 찾으세요.   » Find it on the Internet.
이메일로 파일을 보내요.   » Send the file by Internet.
검은색으로 할게요.   » I'll take the black one.
비싼 것으로 사세요.   » Buy the expensive one.
그걸로 주세요.   » Give me that one please.
맥주로 주세요.   » I'll go with a beer please.
오른쪽으로 가세요.   » Take a right please.
왼쪽으로 가세요.   » Take a left please.
학교로 갈 거예요.   » I'm going to work.
러시아로 가요.   » I'm going to Russia.

»Section 6

Chapter 21

그 사람은 아주 바쁜 사람이에요.   » He is a very busy person.
조용한 생활이 좋아요.   » A quiet lifestyle is comfortable.
큰 집에서 살아요.   » I live in a big house.
인기 많은 프로그램이에요.   » That is a very popular program.

짧은 치마 많이 입어요.   ≫ Short skirts are trendy.

괜찮은 사람이에요.   ≫ He's a good man.

고기 없는 비빔밥 주세요.   ≫ Please give me a bibimpap with no meat.

멋있는 옷이에요.   ≫ Those are cool-looking (stylish) clothes.

맛있는 집이에요.   ≫ That place is delicious.

어려운 질문이에요.   ≫ That's a difficult question.

한국에 매운 음식이 많아요.   ≫ There is a lot of spicy food in Korea.

힘든 일이에요.   ≫ That's a difficult job/thing to deal with.

단 음식을 좋아해요.   ≫ I like sweets.

어떤 사람이 좋아요?   ≫ What kind of person do you like?

어떤 프로를 볼 거예요?   ≫ What kind of program are you going to watch?

어떤 곳이에요?   ≫ What kind of place is it?

Chapter 22

남자 친구에게 쓴 이메일이 길었어요.   ≫ The letter I wrote to my boyfriend was long.

오늘 탄 비행기가 복잡했어요.   ≫ The plane we rode today was crowded.

백화점에서 산 신발이 마음에 안 들어요.   ≫ I don't like the shoes I bought at the department store.

아침에 먹은 계란이 맛이 있었어요.   ≫ The eggs we had this morning were delicious.

어제 읽은 책이 좋았어요.   ≫ The book I read yesterday was good.

민호가 신은 운동화가 멋있어요.   ≫ The gym shoes Minho wore are cool.

치마를 입은 여자가 섹시해요.   ≫ Women wearing skirts are sexy.

내가 만든 아이스크림이에요.   ≫ This is ice cream I made myself.

친구에게 판 차가 좋았어요.   ≫ The car that I sold to my friend was good.

같이 걸은 바닷가가 아름다웠어요.   ≫ The beach that we walked together was beautiful.

지금 들은 노래가 누구 노래예요?   ≫ Whose song is that one we just heard?

이게 내가 들은 이야기예요.   ≫ This is a story/rumor I heard.

Chapter 23

그건 내가 모르는 단어예요.   ≫ That's a word I don't know.

우리가 타는 버스가 몇 번이에요?   ≫ What number is the bus we are riding?

저기서 자는 아이가 예뻐요.   » The baby sleeping over there is pretty.

지금 하는 숙제가 어려워요.   » The homework we are doing is difficult.

걷는 운동이 좋아요.   » Walking is a good form of exercise.
      (lit: Walking exercise is good.)

지금 읽는 책이 재미있어요.   » The book I'm reading is fun/interesting.

지금 찾는 것이 뭐예요?   » What are you looking for?

먹는 것이 아니에요.   » That's not edible.

춤을 추는 것이 싫어요.   » I don't like dancing.

영어를 잘 하는 것이 중요해요.   » Speaking English well is important.

9시간 자는 것은 건강에 안 좋아요. » Sleeping 9 hours is not good for your health.

지금 사는 곳이 어디예요?   » Where is the place you're living?

신문 파는 곳은 어디예요?   » Where is a place that sells newspapers?

잘 만드는 음식이 뭐예요?   » What is the food you are making?

Chapter 24

지금 부를 노래가 한국 노래예요.   » The song I'm going to sing is a Korean song.

내일 볼 공연이 재미있어요.   » The performance we're going to see tomorrow is entertaining.

여행할 나라의 돈이 있어요?   » Do you have money of the country you are traveling to?

신을 등산화를 잊지 마세요.   » Don't forget the hiking shoes you're going to wear.

먹을 것 좀 사서 가요.   » Buy some stuff to eat.

받을 편지가 우체국에 있어요.   » The letter I'm going to get is at the post office.

들을 음악이 없어요.   » I don't have any music to listen to.

입을 옷이 없어요.   » I don't have anything to wear.

먹을 것이 많아요.   » There's a lot to eat.

갈 곳이 없어요.   » There's no place to go.

할 일이 많아요.   » I don't have anything to do.

밥 먹을 시간이 없어요.   » There's no time to eat.

영화 볼 생각이에요.   » I'm thinking about seeing a movie.

Chapter 25

전화하시겠어요?	▶▶ Could you call please?
빨간 신발로 하시겠어요?	▶▶ Would you like to go with the red shoes?
괜찮으시겠어요?	▶▶ Would that be okay?
전화 지금 받으시겠어요?	▶▶ Would you answer the phone now please?
전화 잘못 거셨어요.	▶▶ You dialed the wrong number.
교수님께서 중국에 가셨어요.	▶▶ The professor went to China.
할머니께서 일을 많이 하셨어요.	▶▶ Grandma did a lot of work.
우리 아버지께서 그 책을 읽으셨어요.	▶▶ My father read that book.
삼촌이 월급을 받으실 거예요.	▶▶ My uncle is going to get his salary.
아버지께서 돈이 있으실 거예요.	▶▶ My father will have money.
금방 가실 거예요.	▶▶ They're going to leave soon.
쉬실 거예요?	▶▶ Are you going to rest?

Chapter 26

안녕히 가세요.	▶▶ Good bye. (lit: Go in peace.)
전화 좀 받으세요.	▶▶ Answer the phone please.
쉬세요.	▶▶ Rest. / Relax.
늦지 마세요.	▶▶ Don't be late.
가지 마세요.	▶▶ Don't go.
치마를 입지 마세요.	▶▶ Don't wear a skirt.
안녕하세요?	▶▶ Hello. (lit: Are you peaceful?)
바쁘세요?	▶▶ Are you busy?
추우세요?	▶▶ Are you cold?
그 의사 선생님이 멋있으세요.	▶▶ That doctor is handsome/cool-looking.
할머니께서 지금 청소하세요.	▶▶ Grandma is cleaning.
현욱 씨는 자주 웃으세요.	▶▶ Hyun-ook laughs/smiles a lot.
몇 살이세요?	▶▶ How old are you?
처음이세요?	▶▶ Is it your first time?
의사세요?	▶▶ Are you a doctor?

진지 드셨어요?	▸ Did you have breakfast/lunch/dinner?
학교에 계셨어요?	▸ Did she/he go to school?
선생님 댁이 어디세요?	▸ Where is your house?
푹 주무세요.	▸ Sleep well.
할머니께서 주무세요.	▸ Grandma is sleeping.
할아버지께서 말씀하셨어요.	▸ Grandpa said so.
아버지께서 아직 진지를 드시지 않았어요.	▸ Dad still hasn't eaten yet.
어머니께서 집에 안 계세요.	▸ Mom isn't going/hasn't gone home.
그분께 말씀을 드렸어요.	▸ I told her/him.
선생님 댁에 갔어요.	▸ I went to my/our teacher's house.
할아버지 연세가 많지 않으세요?	▸ Is your grandfather old?
성함이 어떻게 되세요?	▸ What is your name?
연세가 어떻게 되세요?	▸ How old are you?
가족이 어떻게 되세요?	▸ Who is in your family?

▸▸Section 8

침대에 누워요.	▸ Lay on the bed.
도와주세요.	▸ Help me, please.
나는 사장님이 미워요.	▸ I hate the owner.
추우세요?	▸ Are you cold?
한국말이 쉬워요.	▸ Korean is easy.
가까워요?	▸ Is it nearby?
국이 싱거워요.	▸ The broth is bland.

못 들었어요.	▸ I haven't heard that.
친구한테 물어보세요.	▸ Ask a friend.
그 여자 이름을 물었어요?	▸ Did you ask her name?

매일 집까지 걸어요.　　　　　　　　　　» I walk home every day.
들으셨어요?　　　　　　　　　　　　　　» Did you hear?

Chapter 30

지하철이 더 빨라요.　　　　　　　　　　» The subway is faster.
노래를 불렀어요.　　　　　　　　　　　　» I sang a song.
몰랐어요.　　　　　　　　　　　　　　　　» I didn't know that. / I had no idea.

Chapter 31

자주 편지를 써요.　　　　　　　　　　　　» I write letters often.
배가 고파요.　　　　　　　　　　　　　　　» I'm hungry.
저 여자가 예뻐요.　　　　　　　　　　　　» That woman is pretty.
우리 형이 아주 바빠요.　　　　　　　　　　» My older brother is very busy.

Chapter 32

우는 사람이 누구예요?　　　　　　　　　　» Who is the person crying?
내가 사는 동네가 조용해요.　　　　　　　　» The area I'm living in is quiet.
재미있게 노세요.　　　　　　　　　　　　　» Have fun.
먼 곳에 갔어요.　　　　　　　　　　　　　　» She went to a far away place.
단 음식이 싫어요.　　　　　　　　　　　　　» I hate sweet foods.
머리가 긴 여자가 아름다워요.　　　　　　　» Women with long hair are beautiful.

Skills Building Answer Key

▸▸Section 1

Chapter 1 p.27

가 1. ㄷ

여기가 어디예요? 백화점이에요?
아니요, 백화점이 아니에요.
시장이에요.

2. ㄱ

이게 뭐예요?
불고기예요. 아주 맛있어요.

3. ㄱ

이게 녹차예요?
아니요, 커피예요.

4. ㄷ

여기가 은행이에요?
네, 여기가 은행이에요.

나 1. 영화관이에요
2. 회사예요
3. 백화점이에요
4. 학교예요
5. 병원이에요

다 1. 책이에요
2. 기차표예요
3. 김치찌개예요
4. 술이에요
5. 연필이에요

라 1. ㄱ. 의자가 아니에요
　　ㄴ. 책상이에요
2. ㄱ. 시장이 아니에요
　　ㄴ. 백화점이에요

3. ㄱ. 하얀색이 아니에요
　　ㄴ. 파란색이에요
4. ㄱ. 닭갈비가 아니에요
　　ㄴ. 불고기예요
5. ㄱ. 기차역이 아니에요
　　ㄴ. 지하철역이에요

마 1. (ㄱ) 아니요, 녹차가 아니에요.
　　홍차예요
2. (ㅂ) 운동화예요
3. (ㄹ) 우체국이에요
4. (ㄴ) 아니요, 기차역이에요
5. (ㄷ) 네, 화장실이에요
6. (ㅁ) 아니요, 돼지고기예요

Chapter 2 p.33

가 1. ㄱ

이 영화 어때요? 재미있어요?
네, 아주 재미있어요.

2. ㄷ

내일 일해요?
아니요, 집에서 쉬어요.

3. ㄱ

뭘 해요?
책이 없어요. 책을 찾아요.

나 1. 지루해요
2. 좋아요
3. 만나요
4. 다녀요
5. 마셔요
6. 배워요

다 1. 재미있어요
    2. 재미없어요
    3. 힘들어요
    4. 재미있어요
    5. 지루해요
    6. 재미없어요

라 1. 친구를 만나요 - 친구를 자주
       만나요
    2. 영화를 봐요 - 영화를 가끔 봐요
    3. 술을 마셔요 - 술을 가끔 마셔요
    4. 쉬어요 - 가끔 쉬어요
    5. 청소해요 - 청소를 자주 해요
    6. 운동해요 - 운동을 자주 해요

Chapter 3　p.39

가 1. ㄱ
🔊   주말에 뭐 했어요?
       집에서 쉬었어요.
    2. ㄴ
       어제 어디에 갔어요?
       친구하고 공원에 갔어요.
    3. ㄴ
       어디에서 왔어요?
       영국에서 왔어요.

나 1. 아침 7시(일곱 시)에 유식이는
       등산했어요
    2. 아침 11시(열한 시)에 유식이는
       도서관에서 책을 읽었어요
    3. 오후 1시(한 시)에 유식이는
       친구를 만났어요
    4. 오후 2시(두 시)에 영화를 봤어요
    5. 오후 4시(네 시)에 쇼핑했어요
    6. 오후 5시(다섯 시)에 친구하고
       차를 마셨어요

다 1. 시간이 없었어요
    2. 계란을 먹었어요
    3. 비가 왔어요
    4. 기분이 좋았어요
    5. 푹 쉬었어요
    6. 운동 많이 했어요

라 1. 했어요   ㄹ. 숙제요.
    2. 갔어요   ㅂ. 백화점요.
    3. 먹었어요   ㅁ. 비빔밥요.
    4. 만났어요   ㄷ. 선생님요.
    5. 마셨어요   ㄱ. 콜라요.
    6. 도착했어요   ㄴ. 9시요.

Chapter 4　p.45

가 3 → 6 → 2 → 1 → 4 → 5
🔊 이번 주말에 지혜는 청소를 할 거예요.
    그리고 샤워할 거예요. 그리고 친구를
    만날 거예요. 그리고 친구하고 영화를
    볼 거예요. 그리고 차를 마실 거예요.
    그리고 집에서 TV를 볼 거예요.

나 1. 주말에 유식이는 부모님께
       전화할 거예요
    2. 주말에 지혜는 요리할 거예요
    3. 주말에 유식이는 음악을
       들을 거예요
    4. 주말에 지혜는 사진을 찍을 거예요
    5. 주말에 유식이는 공부할 거예요
    6. 주말에 지혜는 쇼핑할 거예요

다 1. 전화할 거예요
    2. 점심을 먹을 거예요
    3. 날씨가 더울 거예요
    4. 부산에 도착할 거예요
    5. 편지를 쓸 거예요
    6. 도서관에 갈 거예요

라 1. (비가) 안 올 거예요
2. (사람이) 많을 거예요
3. (그 사람이 이것을) 좋아할 거예요
4. (그 식당 음식이) 맛없을 거예요
5. (그 영화가) 재미있을 거예요
6. (그 친구가) 안 올 거예요

마 1. 녹차를 마실 거예요
2. 서점에 갈 거예요
3. KTX로 갈 거예요
4. 6시에 갈 거예요
5. 금요일에 전화할 거예요
6. 등산할 거예요

Chapter 5　p.51

가 1. ㄱ
　 주말에 뭘 하겠어요?
　 친구를 만나겠어요.
　 2. ㄴ
　 내일은 춥겠습니까?
　 네, 내일은 눈이 오겠습니다.
　 3. ㄴ
　 내일 등산하시겠어요?
　 아니요, 영화를 보겠어요.

나 1. 맑겠습니다
2. 춥겠습니다
3. 눈이 오겠습니다
4. 덥겠습니다
5. 비가 오겠습니다
6. 흐리겠습니다

다 1. 이따가 전화하겠습니다
2. 비빔밥을 먹겠습니다
3. 아니요, 모르겠습니다

4. 제가 노래하겠습니다
5. 녹차를 마시겠습니다
6. 제가 가겠습니다

라 1. 5시표를 예매하시겠어요
2. 내일 등산하시겠어요
3. 그것을 주시겠어요
4. 이 일을 도와주시겠어요
5. 주말에 여행하시겠어요
6. 잠깐 기다리시겠어요

Chapter 6　p.57

가 1. ㄷ
　 지금 뭘 하고 있어요?
　 지금 방을 청소하고 있어요.
　 2. ㄴ
　 지금 뭐 하고 있어요? 같이
　 영화 봐요.
　 미안해요. 지금 한국어 숙제하고
　 있어요. 시간이 없어요.
　 3. ㄱ
　 어제 아침에 뭐 하고 있었어요?
　 운동하고 있었어요. 날씨가
　 아주 좋았어요.

나 1. 서울 신촌에서 살고 있어요
2. 주말에 축구하고 있어요
3. 요즘 한국말을 배우고 있어요
4. 한국 회사에 다니고 있어요
5. 한국 잡지를 읽고 있어요

다 1. 쓰고 있어요
2. 쓰고 있어요
3. 신고 있어요

4. 차고 있어요
5. 입고 있어요

라
1. 어제 아침 7시에 존은 샤워하고
   있었어요
2. 어제 아침 8시에 존은 지하철을
   타고 있었어요
3. 어제 아침 9시에 존은 인터넷을
   하고 있었어요
4. 어제 오후 1시에 존은 점심을
   먹고 있었어요
5. 어제 저녁 4시에 존은 회의를
   하고 있었어요
6. 어제 저녁 8시에 존은 친구들과
   술을 마시고 있었어요

Chapter 7 p.63

가
1. ㄴ
   내일 시간 있어요?
   아니요, 없어요. 일이 많이 있어요.
2. ㄱ
   집 근처에 백화점이 있어요?
   아니요, 없어요.
   은행은 있어요?
   네, 집 근처에 은행은 있어요.
3. ㄱ
   방에 책상이 있어요?
   네, 책상이 있어요.
   침대도 있어요?
   아니요, 침대는 없어요.

나
1. 병원이 있어요
2. 백화점이 있어요
3. 극장이 없어요
4. 식당이 있어요

5. 약국이 있어요
6. 대학교가 없어요
7. 은행이 있어요

다
1. 돈이 있어요 – 돈이 있어요
2. 내일 시간이 있어요 – 시간이
   없어요
3. 질문이 있어요 – 질문이 없어요
4. 동생이 있어요 – 동생이 있어요
5. 동생이 집에 있어요 – 동생이
   집에 없어요

라
1. 가족이 미국에 있어요
2. 아이가 학교에 있어요
3. 사과가 냉장고에 있어요
4. 은행이 저쪽에 있어요
5. 백화점이 집 근처에 있어요
6. 존이 도서관에 있어요
7. 오빠가 집에 있어요

▶▶Section 2

Chapter 8 p.71

가
1. ㄴ
   이 옷이 어때요?
   좀 커요. 그리고 비싸요. 그런데
   안 예뻐요.
2. ㄴ
   주말에 존하고 같이 등산 갔어요?
   아니요, 존은 안 갔어요.
3. ㄴ
   오늘 날씨가 어때요? 추워요?
   아니요, 안 추워요. 바람이 조금
   불어요.

나
1. 강남역에 안 가요
2. 공부 안 해요
3. 제주도로 여행 안 가요
4. 키가 안 커요
5. 안 피곤해요

다
1. 아직 도착 안 했어요
2. 아직 숙제 안 했어요
3. 아직 전화 안 했어요
4. 아직 집에 안 왔어요
5. 아직 저녁 안 먹었어요

라
1. 운동 안 할 거예요
2. TV 안 볼 거예요
3. 요리 안 할 거예요
4. 술 안 마실 거예요
5. 커피 안 마실 거예요
6. 청소 안 할 거예요
7. 학교에 안 갈 거예요

Chapter 9 p.77

가
1. ㄷ
유식이 생일파티에 누가 왔어요?
존하고 스티븐이 왔어요.
메리는 오지 않았어요.
2. ㄱ
무슨 음식을 좋아해요?
비빔밥하고 불고기를 좋아해요.
그런데 김치는 먹지 않아요.
너무 매워요.
3. ㄱ
이 티셔츠 너무 작지 않아요?
아주 작아요.
이 바지는요?
너무 커요.

나
1. 너무 맵지 않아요
2. 너무 크지 않아요
3. 너무 많지 않아요
4. 너무 늦지 않아요
5. 너무 어렵지 않아요

다
1. 청소하지 않을 거예요
2. 운동하지 않을 거예요
3. 영화보지 않을 거예요
4. 운전하지 않을 거예요
5. 생일 파티에 가지 않을 거예요
6. 회사에 가지 않을 거예요
7. 스키 타지 않을 거예요

라
1. 아니요, 지난 주말에 제주도에
가지 않았어요. 부산에 갔어요
2. 아니요, 비행기로 가지 않았어요.
기차로 갔어요
3. 아니요, 시내에 가지 않았어요.
바닷가에 갔어요
4. 아니요, 사람이 적지 않았어요.
아주 많았어요
5. 아니요, 날씨가 따뜻하지 않았어요.
아주 더웠어요

Chapter 10 p.83

가
1. ㄷ
어디에 주차해요?
은행 옆에 주차하지 마세요.
식당 옆에 주차하세요.
2. ㄴ
유식 씨, 오늘 밤에 전화할까요?
아니요, 존 씨. 오늘 밤에 전화하지
마세요. 내일 제가 전화하겠어요.
3. ㄷ
버스를 탈까요?
버스 타지 마세요. 차가 너무 많아요.
지하철을 타세요.

나 1. 울지 마세요
     2. 담배를 피우지 마세요
     3. 학교에 늦게 오지 마세요
     4. 자지 마세요
     5. 영어로 말하지 마세요

다 1. U턴하지 마세요
     2. 담배 피우지 마세요
     3. 사진 찍지 마세요
     4. 먹지 마세요
     5. 자전거 타지 마세요

라 1. 버스 타지 마
     2. 걱정하지 마. / 걱정 마
     3. 잊지 마
     4. 늦게 전화하지 마
     5. 일찍 가지 마

▶▶Section 3

Chapter 11 p.91

가 1. ㄴ
🔊   내일 누가 와요?
     유식 씨 동생이 와요.
    2. ㄷ
     날씨가 좋아요?
     지금 비가 와요.
    3. ㄷ
     정원에 나무가 많아요. 꽃이
     많이 있어요. 정원이 아주 예뻐요.

나 1. 여자 친구가 와요
     2. 비빔밥이 맛있어요
     3. 형이 운전해요
     4. 영화가 재미있어요

     5. 비가 와요
     6. 시계가 멋있어요

다 1. 한국 노래가 좋아요
     2. 이 식당 음식이 맛있어요
     3. 머리가 아파요
     4. 가방이 좋아요
     5. 동생이 자요
     6. 신발이 예뻐요

라 1. 형이 와요
     2. 누나가 공부해요
     3. 책이 재미있어요
     4. 일이 힘들어요
     5. 일본이 가까워요
     6. 스티븐이 미국 사람이에요

Chapter 12 p.97

가 1. ㄱ
🔊   뭘 먹어요?
     피자를 먹어요. 그리고 콜라를
     마셔요. 맛있어요.
    2. ㄴ
     일요일에 뭐 할 거예요?
     친구를 만날 거예요. 같이 영화를
     볼 거예요.
    3. ㄷ
     잠을 잘 거예요?
     아니요, 숙제를 할 거예요.

나 1. 잠을 자요
     2. 테니스를 쳐요
     3. 사진을 찍어요
     4. 커피를 마셔요
     5. 편지를 써요
     6. 축구를 해요

다
1. 갈비를 좋아해요
2. 감기약을 먹어요
3. 영화를 봐요
4. 음악을 들어요
5. 친구를 만나요
6. 사진을 찍어요

라
1. 형을 기다려요
2. 누나를 만나요
3. 맥주를 마실 거예요
4. 한국 영화를 볼 거예요
5. 축구를 할 거예요
6. 한국말을 배워요

Chapter 13 p.103

가
1. ㄴ
유식 씨는 회사원이에요?
아니요, 저는 선생님이에요.

2. ㄴ
안녕하세요? 저는 중국 사람이에요.
한국대학교에서 공부해요.

3. ㄷ
사과를 샀어요?
아니요, 안 샀어요. 너무 비쌌어요.
배는 두 개 샀어요.

나
1. 저는 선생님이에요. 이분은
회사원이에요
2. 어머니는 책을 봐요. 아버지는
TV를 봐요
3. 동생은 자요. 형은 공부해요
4. 사과는 비싸요. 딸기는 싸요
5. 이분은 유식 씨예요. 저분은
존 씨예요
6. 서울은 추워요. 뉴욕은 따뜻해요

다
1. 네, 한국 음식을 좋아해요. 냉면은
안 좋아해요
2. 네, 음악을 자주 들어요. 클래식
음악은 안 들어요
3. 네, 꽃을 샀어요.
케이크는 안 샀어요
4. 네, 가방을 살 거예요. 구두는
안 살 거예요
5. 네, 이 영화를 볼 거예요. 저 영화는
안 볼 거예요
6. 네, 동생을 만나요. 형은 안 만나요

라
1. 네, 그렇지만 편의점에서는 안 팔아요
2. 네, 그렇지만 어제 숙제는 안 쉬웠어요
3. 네, 그렇지만 북경은 안 추워요
4. 네, 그렇지만 집에서는 안 피워요
5. 네, 그렇지만 저 책은 재미없어요
6. 네, 그렇지만 저 식당 음식은 맛없어요

▶▶Section 4

Chapter 14 p.111

가
1. ㄱ
저녁 때 뭐 먹을 거예요?
콜라랑 피자 먹을 거예요.

2. ㄴ
켈리 씨는 한국어를 잘 해요?
아니요, 그런데 중국어하고
일본어는 잘 해요.

3. ㄴ
어제 백화점에 누구랑 갔어요?
동생이랑 갔어요. 동생이 옷이랑
구두를 샀어요.

나
1. 사과랑 딸기를 사요. / 사과하고
   딸기를 사요. / 사과와 딸기를 사요
2. 일본이랑 중국을 여행해요. / 일본하고
   중국을 여행해요. / 일본과 중국을
   여행해요
3. 백화점이랑 은행이 있어요. / 백화
   점하고 은행이 있어요. / 백화점과
   은행이 있어요
4. 어머니랑 쇼핑해요. / 어머니하고
   쇼핑해요. / 어머니와 쇼핑해요
5. 친구랑 학교에 가요. / 친구하고
   학교에 가요. / 친구와 학교에 가요
6. 운동화랑 구두를 사요. / 운동화하고
   구두를 사요. / 운동화와 구두를
   사요

다
1. 시장에서 사과하고 배를 샀어요
2. 백화점에서 가방하고 시계를 살
   거예요
3. 다음 주에 제주도하고 부산을
   여행할 거예요
4. 회사에 지하철하고 버스로 가요
5. 여기에 이름하고 주소를 쓰세요
6. 다음 주말에 승주하고 마이클을
   만나요

라
1. 기차하고 배로 갔어요
2. 넥타이랑 지갑을 샀어요
3. 베트남하고 캄보디아를
   여행할 거예요
4. 동생과 동생 여자 친구가 집에
   왔어요
5. 동생하고 영화를 볼 거예요
6. 앞집 아줌마랑 싸웠어요

Chapter 15 p. 117

가
1. ㄴ
   유식이 생일에 무슨 선물을
   줄 거예요?
   영화표나 음악 CD를 줄 거예요.
2. ㄷ
   시간이 있으면 보통 뭐 해요?
   수영이나 등산해요.
3. ㄴ
   우리 차 한잔해요.
   좋아요.
   무슨 차 마셔요?
   녹차나 홍차 마실게요.

나
1. 콜라나 오렌지 주스를 마셔요
2. 등산이나 쇼핑을 해요
3. 중국이나 일본을 여행해요
4. 토요일이나 일요일에 파티를 해요
5. 지갑이나 장갑을 줘요
6. 축구나 야구를 해요

다
1. 불고기나 라면을
2. 맥주나 와인을
3. 운동이나 서울 구경을
4. 이번 주말이나 다음 주말에
5. 구두나 옷을
6. 영어 공부나 일어 공부를

라
1. 전화나 이메일로 연락해요
2. 한국 영화나 일본 영화를
   볼 거예요
3. 시장이나 백화점에서 사요
4. 영화나 공연을 봐요
5. 비디오나 볼 거예요
6. 여행이나 할 거예요

가 1. ㄱ
🔊 저 식당은 값이 싸요?
아니요, 음식도 맛없고요.
2. ㄴ
메리 씨는 한국에 갔어요?
네, 중국에도 갔어요. 일본에
아직 안 갔어요.
3. ㄴ
어제 유식 씨 생일 파티에 존 씨가
왔어요?
네, 영숙 씨도 왔어요. 하지만
메리 씨는 안 왔어요.

나 1. 저도 쉬었어요
2. 제 동생도 키가 작아요
3. 저도 노래를 좋아해요
4. 저도 숙제를 안 했어요
5. 저도 자전거를 못 타요
6. 우리 형도 주말에 등산해요

다 1. 은
도
2. 도
는
3. 는
도
4. 도
도

라 1. 대학교에서 한국어를 배워요
대학교에서 한국어를 안 배워요
2. 영화를 좋아해요
영화를 안 좋아해요
3. 도서관에 가지 않아요
도서관에 가지 않아요

4. 추워요
안 추울 거예요

가 1. ㄷ
🔊 이건 누구 차예요? 켈리 어머니
거예요?
아니요, 켈리 동생 거예요. 아주
좋아요.
2. ㄷ
저분이 누구예요?
영숙 씨 남편이에요. 영숙 씨
남편은 제 친구예요.
3. ㄱ
이 휴대전화는 누구 거예요?
내 거예요. 유식 씨 거하고 같아요.

나 1. 유식 씨의 책이에요
2. 존 씨의 안경이에요
3. 마이클의 자전거예요
4. 영숙이의 가방이에요
5. 메리의 휴대전화예요

다 1. 저의/제 책이에요
2. 나의/내 지갑이에요
3. 존의/존 집이에요
4. 재운이의/재운이 부인이에요
5. 메리의/메리 어머니예요

라 1. 이건 메리 컴퓨터예요. / 이건
메리 거예요
2. 이건 유식이 안경이에요. / 이건
유식이 거예요
3. 저건 존 휴대전화예요. / 저건
존 거예요
4. 저건 영숙이 차예요. / 저건
영숙이 거예요

5. 이건 윌슨 잡지예요. / 이건
   윌슨 거예요

▶▶Section 5

가
1. ㄴ
   이게 뭐예요?
   옷이에요.
   누구한테 줄 거예요?
   부모님께 드릴 거예요.
2. ㄱ
   저는 요즘 한국말을 가르쳐요.
   누구한테요?
   미국 사람한테요.
3. ㄱ
   누구한테 전화해요?
   친구한테요.
   왜요?
   이번 주말에 우리 집에서 파티를
   해요.

나
1. 유식 씨가 정희한테/정희에게
   전화해요
2. 유식 씨가 정희한테/정희에게
   선물을 줘요
3. 유식 씨가 정희한테/정희에게
   꽃을 줘요
4. 유식 씨가 부모님께 편지를 써요
5. 유식 씨가 선생님께 질문을 해요

다
1. 어제 언니한테 전화했어요
2. 남자 친구한테 편지를 썼어요

3. 부모님께 선물을 보냈어요
4. 선생님께 질문했어요
5. 외국 사람한테 한국말이 어려워요

라
1. 누구한테 이 선물을 줄 거예요
2. 누구한테 전화할 거예요
3. 누구한테 옷을 줘요
4. 그 사진이 누구한테 있어요
5. 누구한테 한국말을 가르쳐요

가
1. ㄱ
   유식 씨, 지금 어디에 있어요?
   친구 집에 있어요.
2. ㄴ
   주말에 어디에 갔어요?
   동생하고 설악산에 갔어요.
3. ㄱ
   유식 씨, 제 가방 봤어요?
   네, 책상 위에 있어요.

나
1. 지혜 씨가 도서관에 가요
2. 지혜 씨가 우체국에 가요
3. 지혜 씨가 영화관에 가요
4. 지혜 씨가 커피숍에 가요

다
1. 지혜 씨가 도서관에서 책을 읽어요
2. 지혜 씨가 우체국에서 편지를
   보내요
3. 지혜 씨가 영화관에서 영화를 봐요
4. 지혜 씨가 커피숍에서 커피를 마셔요

라
1. 누나가 집에 있어요
2. 언니가 회사에 갔어요
3. 한국 노래를 노래방에서 불렀어요
4. 주말에 집에서 쉬었어요

5. 제 친구가 미국에서 왔어요
6. 영화가 5시에 시작해요

마 1. 자동차 회사에서 일해요
2. 명동에 갔어요
3. 독일에서 왔어요
4. 광화문에 있어요
5. 다음 주 화요일에 와요
6. 헬스장에서 운동해요

바 1. 책상 위에 열쇠가 있어요
2. 창문 앞에 책상이 있어요
3. 열쇠 옆에 안경이 있어요
4. 침대 밑에 구두가 있어요
5. 책상하고 침대 사이에 가방이 있어요
6. 책상 뒤에 창문이 있어요

Chapter 20 p.149

가 1. ㄱ
회사에 어떻게 가요?
지하철로 가요. 지하철이 빨라요.
2. ㄴ
메리 씨는 유식 씨한테 한국말로
말해요?
아니요, 영어로 말해요.
한국말로는 아직 어려워요.
3. ㄱ
커피하고 우유하고 콜라가 있어요.
뭐 드시겠어요?
우유로 주세요.

나 1. 학교에 자전거로 가요
2. 회사에 버스로 가요
3. 영어로 말해요
4. 기차로 여행해요
5. 디카(디지털 카메라)로
사진을 찍어요

다 1. 한국 사람은 수저로 밥을 먹어요
2. 친구하고 일본어로 말해요
3. 이게 한국말로 뭐예요
4. 그 사람을 처음으로 만났어요
5. 회사에 지하철로 다녀요

라 1. 비행기로 왔어요
2. 기차로 갔어요
3. 빨간색으로 하겠어요
4. 집으로 가요
5. 한국어로 말해요

>>**Section 6**

Chapter 21 p.157

가 1. ㄷ
유식 씨 누나가 누구예요?
저기 머리가 짧은 사람이에요.
2. ㄱ
유식 씨 집이 어디예요?
저기 큰 집이에요. 집 앞에 차가
있어요.
3. ㄴ
유식 씨는 더운 날씨를
좋아해요?
아니요, 추운 날씨를 좋아해요.

나 1. 키가 큰 남자가 좋아요
2. 키가 작은 남자가 좋아요
3. 추운 날씨가 좋아요
4. 더운 날씨가 좋아요
5. 매운 음식이 좋아요
6. 단 음식이 좋아요

다
1. 재미있는 영화였어요
2. 키가 큰 사람이에요
3. 복잡한 시장이에요
4. 단 음식을 좋아해요
5. 아름다운 산이에요

라
1. 친절한
2. 매운
3. 맛있는
4. 비싼
5. 어려운

Chapter 22 p.163

가
1. ㄴ
어제 만난 사람이 누구예요?
어제 존하고 영숙이를 만났어요.
2. ㄴ
어제 간 극장이 어디에 있어요?
한국서점 옆에 있어요.
3. ㄷ
유식이가 좋아한 사람이
영숙이예요?
아니요, 존이 좋아한 사람이
영숙이예요. 그런데 영숙이는
유식이를 좋아했어요.

나
1. 간
2. 읽은
3. 먹은
4. 본
5. 받은

다
1. 어제 마신 커피는 4,000원이었어요
2. 주말에 등산한 산은
관악산이에요
3. 어제 만난 친구는 존이에요
4. 지난 금요일에 본 영화가 재미있었어요

5. 어제 산 신발이 마음에 안 들어요

라
1. 유식이의 생일에 온 사람은
나하고 존하고 마이클이에요
2. 늦게 온 사람은 마이클이에요
3. 내가 유식이한테 준 선물은
생일 카드와 CD예요
4. 존이 유식이한테 준 선물은
생일 케이크예요
5. 유식이가 만든 음식은
한국 음식이에요

Chapter 23 p.169

가
1. ㄱ
지금 마시는 차가 뭐예요?
커피예요. 수잔 씨, 그 차는
무슨 차예요?
이건 제가 자주 마시는 녹차예요.
2. ㄷ
무슨 운동을 좋아해요?
전 걷는 운동이 좋아요.
3. ㄷ
부산으로 가는 비행기는
몇 시에 출발해요?
오전 11시요.
도착하는 시간은요?
12시예요.

나
1. 책을 읽는 사람이 존이에요
2. 사과를 먹는 사람이 유식이에요
3. 웃는 사람이 영숙이에요
4. 춤을 추는 사람이 마이클이에요
5. 전화를 하는 사람이 수잔이에요

다
1. 하는
2. 좋아하는
3. 웃는

4. 사는
5. 파는
6. 만드는

라 1. 영숙이가 여행하는 곳은
제주도예요
2. 유식이가 다니는 회사는
우리 집에서 가까워요
3. 존이 사귀는 여자 친구는
한국 사람이에요
4. 수잔이 마시는 차는 녹차예요
5. 마이클 씨가 만나는 친구는
메리예요

Chapter 24 p.175

가 1. ㄴ
영숙이한테 줄 생일 선물이 뭐예요?
영숙이는 음악을 좋아해요. CD를
줄 거예요. 그리고 꽃도 줄 거예요.
2. ㄱ
메리 씨, 오늘 만날 사람이 누구예요?
유식 씨하고 존 씨예요.
영숙 씨도 만날 거예요?
아니요, 영숙씨는 내일 만날 거예요.
3. ㄱ
내일 등산에 마실 물하고 따뜻한
옷을 준비해요.
먹을 음식도 준비해요?
네, 먹을 음식도 준비해요.

나 1. 친구에게 줄 선물은 꽃이에요
2. 지금 탈 KTX는 부산에 가요
3. 시장에서 살 과일은 사과하고
바나나예요
4. 냉장고 안에 먹을 것이 없어요

5. 우리 가족이 같이 살 집은
큰 집이에요

다 1. 영숙이가 여행할 곳은 제주도예요
2. 유식이가 다닐 회사는 작은
회사예요
3. 존이 메리한테 줄 선물은 꽃이에요
4. 수잔이 만들 한국 음식은
비빔밥이에요
5. 마이클이 만날 친구는 메리예요

라 1. 들을 음악이 없어요
2. 오늘 배울 단어가 뭐예요
3. 문 닫을 시간이에요
4. 먹을 것 좀 사요
5. 내릴 문은 오른쪽입니다
6. 여행할 시간이 없어요

▶▶Section 7

Chapter 25 p.183

가 1. ㄱ
어서 오세요. 뭘 주문하시겠어요?
커피 하나하고 오렌지 주스 하나요.
죄송합니다. 오렌지 주스가 없어요.
그럼 커피 둘 주세요.
2. ㄴ
유식 씨, 오늘 뭐 하실 거예요?
인사동에 갈 거예요.
혼자 가실 거예요?
아니요, 아버지도 같이 가실 거예요.
3. ㄴ
교수님은 어디에 가셨어요?
중국에 가셨어요.

언제 가셨어요?
어제요.

나 1. 어머니께서 시장에 가셨어요
2. 어머니께서 쇼핑하셨어요
3. 아버지께서 책을 읽으셨어요
4. 아버지께서 텔레비전을 보셨어요
5. 할아버지께서 등산하셨어요
6. 아버지께서 운전하셨어요

다 1. 차 한잔하시겠어요
2. 뭐 주문하시겠어요
3. 무슨 영화 보시겠어요
4. 지하철을 타시겠어요? 버스를
   타시겠어요
5. 무슨 색을 사시겠어요
6. 어디에 가시겠어요

라 1. 하셨어요
   친구하고 영화를 봤어요
2. 하실 거예요
   등산할 거예요
3. 가실 거예요
   북한산에 갈 거예요
4. 만나실 거예요
   구파발역에서 만날 거예요
5. 하실 거예요
   집에서 쉴 거예요
6. 읽으실 거예요
   한국 잡지를 읽을 거예요

Chapter 26 p.189

가 1. ㄱ
🔊 존 씨 아버지께서는 뭐 하세요?
회사에 다니세요.
어머니는요?
영어 선생님이세요.

2. ㄷ
존 씨, 매일 운동하세요?
아니요, 주말에만 해요.
어디에서 운동하세요?
집 근처 헬스장에서요.
3. ㄴ
안녕하세요? 유식 씨, 어디 가세요?
학교에 가요. 메리 씨는 어디에 가세요?
저는 커피숍에 가요. 친구를
만날 거예요.

나 1. 한국어를 가르치세요
2. 요리하세요
3. 신문을 보세요
4. 쉬세요
5. 책을 읽으세요
6. 운동하세요

다 1. 차 한잔하시겠어요
2. 지금 무슨 일을 하세요
3. 요즘 회사일이 많으세요
4. 무슨 음식을 좋아하세요
5. 지난 휴가에 뭐 하셨어요
6. 의사 선생님이세요

라 1. 전화하세요 – 전화하지 마세요
2. 기다리세요 – 기다리지 마세요
3. 운동하세요 – 운동하지 마세요
4. 웃으세요 – 웃지 마세요
5. 집에 가세요 – 집에 가지 마세요
6. 책을 읽으세요 – 책을 읽지 마세요

Chapter 27 p.195

가 1. ㄴ
🔊 여보세요? 김 선생님 댁이죠?
네, 그런데요.

저는 김유식인데요, 김 선생님
계세요?
지금 학교에 계세요

2. ㄷ
김 선생님, 점심 드셨어요?
네, 이 선생님은 점심 드셨어요?
저는 지금 먹을 거예요.

3. ㄴ
쉬잇, 조용히 하세요. 지금
할아버지께서 주무세요.
그래요? 할머니께서는 댁에 계세요?
아니요, 안 계세요.

나 1. 교실에 계세요
2. 진지를 드세요
3. 책을 드려요
4. 성함이 김영순이세요
5. 주무세요
6. 연세가 여든이세요

다 1. 안녕히 주무세요
2. 맛있게 드세요. / 많이 드세요
3. 성함이 어떻게 되세요
4. 연세가 어떻게 되세요
5. 안녕히 계세요
6. 점심 드셨어요

라 1. 1월 1일에 우리는 교수님 댁에 갔어요
2. 교수님께서 우리를 초대하셨어요
3. 우리는 교수님께 드릴 꽃을 샀어요
4. 우리는 교수님께 꽃을 드렸어요
5. 교수님께서 "꽃이 아주 예뻐요."라고
말씀(을) 하셨어요
6. 우리는 교수님께 "새해 복 많이
받으세요."라고 말씀(을) 드렸어요

▶▶Section 8

Chapter 28~32 p.211

가 1. ㄷ
요즘 한국 날씨가 어때요?
아주 더워요. 미국은 어때요?
추워요. 가끔 눈도 와요.

2. ㄴ
머리가 긴 사람이 누나예요?
아니요, 키가 큰 사람이
우리 누나예요.

3. ㄱ
영숙 씨, 사는 곳이 어디세요?
여의도예요. 존 씨는요?
제가 사는 곳은 이태원역 근처예요.

나 1. 잘 몰라요
2. 머리가 아파요
3. 부모님께 편지를 써요
4. 노래를 불러요
5. 김치가 매워요
6. 배가 고파요
7. 음악을 들어요
8. 날씨가 더워요

다 1. 우는
2. 단
3. 만든
4. 긴
5. 사세요
6. 아는

라 1. 걸었어요
2. 어려워요
3. 골라요
4. 미세요
5. 커요
6. 몰라요
7. 바빠요
8. 먼

Basic Verb Conjugations

Verb	Meaning	V어(아,여)요	V었(았,였)어요	V(으)ㄹ 거예요
가다	to go	가요	갔어요	갈 거예요
가르치다	to teach	가르쳐요	가르쳤어요	가르칠 거예요
기다리다	to wait	기다려요	기다렸어요	기다릴 거예요
끝나다	to end, finish	끝나요	끝났어요	끝날 거예요
나가다	to go out	나가요	나갔어요	나갈 거예요
나오다	to come out	나와요	나왔어요	나올 거예요
늦다	to be late	늦어요	늦었어요	늦을 거예요
다니다	to attend	다녀요	다녔어요	다닐 거예요
닫다	to close	닫아요	닫았어요	닫을 거예요
도착하다	to arrive	도착해요	도착했어요	도착할 거예요
마시다	to drink	마셔요	마셨어요	마실 거예요
만나다	to meet	만나요	만났어요	만날 거예요
말하다	to speak	말해요	말했어요	말할 거예요
맞다	to fit	맞아요	맞았어요	맞을 거예요
먹다	to eat	먹어요	먹었어요	먹을 거예요
믿다	to believe	믿어요	믿었어요	믿을 거예요
받다	to receive	받아요	받았어요	받을 거예요
배우다	to learn	배워요	배웠어요	배울 거예요
보내다	to send	보내요	보냈어요	보낼 거예요
보다	to see, look at	봐요	봤어요	볼 거예요
사다	to buy	사요	샀어요	살 거예요
샤워하다	to take a shower	샤워해요	샤워했어요	샤워할 거예요
쇼핑하다	to shop	쇼핑해요	쇼핑했어요	쇼핑할 거예요
쉬다	to rest	쉬어요	쉬었어요	쉴 거예요
시작하다	to start	시작해요	시작했어요	시작할 거예요
신다	to put on (foot wear)	신어요	신었어요	신을 거예요
싫어하다	to hate	싫어해요	싫어했어요	싫어할 거예요
싸우다	to fight	싸워요	싸웠어요	싸울 거예요

Verb	Meaning	V어(아,여)요	V었(았,였)어요	V(으)ㄹ 거예요
여행하다	to travel	여행해요	여행했어요	여행할 거예요
연락하다	to contact	연락해요	연락했어요	연락할 거예요
예매하다	to purchase in advance	예매해요	예매했어요	예매할 거예요
오다	to come	와요	왔어요	올 거예요
운전하다	to drive	운전해요	운전했어요	운전할 거예요
웃다	to laugh, smile	웃어요	웃었어요	웃을 거예요
웃기다	to be funny	웃겨요	웃겼어요	웃길 거예요
이야기하다	to talk	이야기해요	이야기했어요	이야기할 거예요
일하다	to work	일해요	일했어요	일할 거예요
읽다	to read	읽어요	읽었어요	읽을 거예요
입다	to wear (clothes)	입어요	입었어요	입을 거예요
잊다	to forget	잊어요	잊었어요	잊을 거예요
자다	to sleep	자요	잤어요	잘 거예요
걱정하다	to worry	걱정해요	걱정했어요	걱정할 거예요
좋아하다	to like	좋아해요	좋아했어요	좋아할 거예요
주다	to give	줘요	줬어요	줄 거예요
주문하다	to make an order	주문해요	주문했어요	주문할 거예요
주차하다	to park a car	주차해요	주차했어요	주차할 거예요
준비하다	to prepare	준비해요	준비했어요	준비할 거예요
찾다	to look for, find	찾아요	찾았어요	찾을 거예요
청소하다	to clean	청소해요	청소했어요	청소할 거예요
출발하다	to depart	출발해요	출발했어요	출발할 거예요
타다	to ride	타요	탔어요	탈 거예요
하다	to do	해요	했어요	할 거예요
'ㅂ' irregular verbs				
눕다	to lie down	누워요	누웠어요	누울 거예요
돕다	to help	도와요	도왔어요	도울 거예요
'ㄷ' irregular verbs				
걷다	to walk	걸어요	걸었어요	걸을 거예요

Verb	Meaning	V어(아,여)요	V었(았,였)어요	V(으)ㄹ 거예요
듣다	to listen, hear	들어요	들었어요	들을 거예요
묻다	to ask	물어요	물었어요	물을 거예요
'르' irregular verbs				
고르다	to choose	골라요	골랐어요	고를 거예요
부르다	to sing (a song), call (somebody)	불러요	불렀어요	부를 거예요
'으' irregular verbs				
쓰다	to write, use, wear to be bitter	써요	썼어요	쓸 거예요
'ㄹ' omission irregular verbs				
놀다	to play	놀아요	놀았어요	놀 거예요
만들다	to make	만들어요	만들었어요	만들 거예요
밀다	to push	밀어요	밀었어요	밀 거예요
살다	to live	살아요	살았어요	살 거예요
알다	to know	알아요	알았어요	알 거예요
불다	to blow	불어요	불었어요	불 거예요
울다	to cry	울어요	울었어요	울 거예요
팔다	to sell	팔아요	팔았어요	팔 거예요
Noun / Verb pairs				
노래를 부르다	to sing a song	노래를 불러요	노래를 불렀어요	노래를 부를 거예요
담배를 피우다	to smoke	담배를 피워요	담배를 피웠어요	담배를 피울 거예요
마음에 들다	to like	마음에 들어요	마음에 들었어요	마음에 들 거예요
사진을 찍다	to take a picture	사진을 찍어요	사진을 찍었어요	사진을 찍을 거예요
시간이 걸리다	to take time	시간이 걸려요	시간이 걸렸어요	시간이 걸릴 거예요
시계를 차다	to wear a watch	시계를 차요	시계를 찼어요	시계를 찰 거예요
춤을 추다	to dance a dance	춤을 춰요	춤을 췄어요	춤을 출 거예요
친구를 사귀다	to make a friend	친구를 사귀어요	친구를 사귀었어요	친구를 사귈 거예요
테니스를 부치다	to play tennis	테니스를 쳐요	테니스를 쳤어요	테니스를 칠 거예요
화가 나다	to be angry	화가 나요	화가 났어요	화가 날 거예요

Basic Adjective Conjugations

Adjectives	Meaning	A어(아,여)요	A었(았,였)어요	A(으)ㄹ 거예요
간단하다	to be simple	간단해요	간단했어요	간단할 거예요
괜찮다	to be okay	괜찮아요	괜찮았어요	괜찮을 거예요
깨끗하다	to be clean	깨끗해요	깨끗했어요	깨끗할 거예요
뚱뚱하다	to be fat	뚱뚱해요	뚱뚱했어요	뚱뚱할 거예요
많다	to be a lot	많아요	많았어요	많을 거예요
맑다	to be sunny	맑아요	맑았어요	맑을 거예요
맛있다	to be delicious	맛있어요	맛있었어요	맛있을 거예요
멋있다	to be stylish	멋있어요	멋있었어요	멋있을 거예요
미안하다	to be sorry	미안해요	미안했어요	미안할 거예요
복잡하다	to be crowded	복잡해요	복잡했어요	복잡할 거예요
비싸다	to be expensive	비싸요	비쌌어요	비쌀 거예요
심심하다	to be bored	심심해요	심심했어요	심심할 거예요
싫다	to hate	싫어요	싫었어요	싫어할 거예요
싸다	to be cheap	싸요	쌌어요	쌀 거예요
작다	to be small	작아요	작았어요	작을 거예요
재미있다	to be interesting, fun	재미있어요	재미있었어요	재미있을 거예요
적다	to be few	적어요	적었어요	적을 거예요
조용하다	to be quiet	조용해요	조용했어요	조용할 거예요
좋다	to be good	좋아요	좋았어요	좋을 거예요
중요하다	to be important	중요해요	중요했어요	중요할 거예요
지루하다	to be boring	지루해요	지루했어요	지루할 거예요
피곤하다	to be tired	피곤해요	피곤했어요	피곤할 거예요
필요하다	to be necessary	필요해요	필요했어요	필요할 거예요
친절하다	to be kind	친절해요	친절했어요	친절할 거예요
행복하다	to be happy	행복해요	행복했어요	행복할 거예요
흐리다	to be cloudy	흐려요	흐렸어요	흐릴 거예요

'ㅂ' irregular adjectives

Adjectives	Meaning	A어(아,여)요	A었(았,였)어요	A(으)ㄹ 거예요
가깝다	to be close	가까워요	가까웠어요	가까울 거예요

Adjectives	Meaning	A어(아,여)요	A었(았,였)어요	A(으)ㄹ 거예요
가볍다	to be light	가벼워요	가벼웠어요	가벼울 거예요
더럽다	to be dirty	더러워요	더러웠어요	더러울 거예요
덥다	to be hot	더워요	더웠어요	더울 거예요
맵다	to be spicy	매워요	매웠어요	매울 거예요
밉다	to hate (somebody)	미워요	미웠어요	미울 거예요
무겁다	to be heavy	무거워요	무거웠어요	무거울 거예요
무섭다	to be scary	무서워요	무서웠어요	무서울 거예요
쉽다	to be easy	쉬워요	쉬웠어요	쉬울 거예요
싱겁다	to be bland	싱거워요	싱거웠어요	싱거울 거예요
어렵다	to be difficult	어려워요	어려웠어요	어려울 거예요
춥다	to be cold	추워요	추웠어요	추울 거예요

'르' irregular adjectives

Adjectives	Meaning	A어(아,여)요	A었(았,였)어요	A(으)ㄹ 거예요
다르다	to be different	달라요	달랐어요	다를 거예요
빠르다	to be fast	빨라요	빨랐어요	빠를 거예요

'으' irregular adjectives

Adjectives	Meaning	A어(아,여)요	A었(았,였)어요	A(으)ㄹ 거예요
배가 고프다	to be hungry	배가 고파요	배가 고팠어요	배가 고플 거예요
나쁘다	to be bad	나빠요	나빴어요	나쁠 거예요
바쁘다	to be busy	바빠요	바빴어요	바쁠 거예요
슬프다	to be sad	슬퍼요	슬펐어요	슬플 거예요
아프다	to be sick	아파요	아팠어요	아플 거예요
예쁘다	to be pretty	예뻐요	예뻤어요	예쁠 거예요
크다	to be big, large	커요	컸어요	클 거예요
키가 크다	to be tall	키가 커요	키가 컸어요	키가 클 거예요

'ㄹ' omission irregular adjectives

Adjectives	Meaning	A어(아,여)요	A었(았,였)어요	A(으)ㄹ 거예요
길다	to be long	길어요	길었어요	길 거예요
달다	to be sweet	달아요	달았어요	달 거예요
멀다	to be far	멀어요	멀었어요	멀 거예요
힘들다	to be draining	힘들어요	힘들었어요	힘들 거예요